Beyond All Limitations

STORIES OF FREEDOM'S LITTLE MIRACLES

Beyond All Limitations

STORIES OF FREEDOM'S LITTLE MIRACLES

NANCY A. KIBUTHU

Produced by Michelle Beckman, CEO of Sunday Dinner Stories, SundayDinnerStories.com

Book design and cover design by Michelle Beckman, CEO of Sunday Dinner Stories, SundayDinnerStories.com

This book is based on interviews conducted by Michelle Beckman of Sunday Dinner Stories with Nancy A. Kibuthu during October 2019.

Beyond All Limitations: Stories of Freedom's Little Miracles
Nancy A. Kibuthu
ISBN-13: 978-0-578-76017-9

For my miracle babies,
Nicole and Jesse:

May you
appreciate freedom's little miracles
and always remember you have no limitations

CONTENTS

ACKNOWLEDGMENTS

To my mom, Florence Njoki Kibuthu: You've always been my hero. You probably have no idea how much you influenced my life, but you will after you read this book. I love you!

To my sisters—Josephine, Grace, and Margaret: You are a constant source of strength for me. Thousands of miles cannot keep us apart. I love you all.

To my baby cousin, Erick: You are a miracle who came into our home at just the right time. I'm so grateful that you've been here for me. I thank God for you and your support, especially during these extremely difficult past two years.

To my sister-in-law, Purity: Thank you for your help. You are always there when I call.

To my Uncle Arch Henry Gatai: Thank you for encouraging me to be me and to work harder. Because of you, I'm no longer afraid to tell my story.

To my husband and love of my life, David Mithamo Nyaguthii: My memories of you will never fade. You believed in me and loved me more than I did myself. You lived your life for our children and me. I will never forget you. We will be together always in our hearts.

David and me

CHAPTER ONE

I AM BLESSED

BUYING A STAMP TO SEND A LETTER to America was not cheap, but I knew if I reached my goal, it would be worth the price of a few saved or borrowed coins. I bought my stamp, wrote my letter, and mailed it. *Dear Reverend Parsley, I would like to come to America. Would you please pray for me?*

Every Sunday, I went to church in my Kenyan village with my mom and my sisters. After church, my uncle Gakuo's mother, Grandma *cucu wa* Mumbi, passed by my house walking barefoot. I would invite her to stay as I warmed up some water to clean her feet.

Excavating the chiggers from my grandma's feet was the hardest part of the pedicure. A chigger is a minute animal, like a flea, if I may call it that. When you walk barefoot, the chiggers attach themselves to your feet and feed on your skin. Their bites are itchy, and most people want to remove the mites as quickly as possible. Some people get used to the irritation and let the chiggers remain until they dislodge on their own. But if you don't regularly clean your feet, you could find yourself in agony.

I was about nine or ten years old when I started this service for my Grandma *cucu w*a Mumbi and my neighbor *cucu wa* Sherina. *Cucu wa* Sherina was only seventy-something years old, but she looked significantly older. I would wash their feet, carefully eliminate the chiggers, add an antibiotic to kill the bacteria, and rub oil on their feet. These women worked hard and deserved a luxurious massage.

My mom and my sisters couldn't understand why I loved blessing these women with pedicures. Neither could the rest of my village. My secret? I cherished hearing the women's stories. They'd talk about when they were little girls, when they met their boyfriends, the dances they attended, and the outfits they wore with pride. I would laugh so hard. Looking back, I think they also served as my personal therapists, in a way. And during my childhood, I looked for happiness and connection in the simplest of activities.

Those women are long gone now, but I remember their stories, and I remember them. Little did I know that those special moments would influence my life and career more than a decade later. As a teenager, I liked to listen to motivational speakers, especially courageous women moving the world with love. My mom was, and up to date is, my hero. My aunties, from both sides of my family, exerted special influence to help guide me down the right path. The businesswomen from the Maendeleo Ya Wanawake organization left me in awe and literally changed my life. Women were my role models back then. You'll hear more about all of them later.

Around the year 2000, I went to see Joyce Meyer, a Christian teacher, in Nairobi. It was about a two-hour drive, and she preached at the Kenyatta International Convention Centre (KICC)—a huge, modern venue in the heart of the city. Everyone who could afford it attended to hear her speak. I remember Joyce saying something like, "You should be fearful of that person who is above. That person is God, and you should know that He has the power, and He's the provider of everything. You should know He loves you."

Joyce spoke about courage. At that time, Kenyans didn't have an abundance of hope, and she wanted to encourage us to go beyond our perceived limitations. I saw a woman who loved God, and I yearned to be that kind of woman. I admired her so much, and to this day, I still do.

During my childhood, I wished I could come to America, but with the exception of writing the letter to the reverend, I really didn't dream about it. I would soon realize, though, that God was working His miracles, and the lessons I learned during Joyce's message of courage would play a pivotal role in my future.

I took many risks by myself before I met my husband, David. Then we took many risks together. David was a kind, understanding, and loving man. Everything he did was for the benefit of our two children and me. He provided everything I'd ever wanted. So when he said, "You should write a book. Your life is very profound, and people should know the kind of a person you are and what has happened in your life," I listened.

He (and I) believed that my story is filled with miracles and, very simply, hard work. I've treasured listening to other people's stories since I was a child. I've learned from inspirational speakers and authors. I've always adored reading. And now it's time for me to write my story in hopes of inspiring my children as well as little girls and boys in Kenya to go beyond their limitations. As I tell my story, you'll also learn about the people who helped me become who I am today.

I went from a little girl voluntarily scraping chiggers off old women's feet to a wife, mother, business owner, and proud Kenyan-American. These days, when I wake up in the morning and see the sun, I'm overwhelmed with joy. I know I'm blessed and grateful to God for my life. I want you to know that you are blessed and can do anything you want to do too.

CHAPTER TWO

THE FREEDOM CROSSWALK

MIRACLES COME IN MANY PACKAGES, but they are easier to spot when they're wrapped in freedom and opened with a humble heart. Twenty years later, I'm still shocked that I live in my own house in a safe neighborhood with exceptional schools in a small town and, most importantly, in America! I always hoped to be here but never thought it would happen. Every day that I wake up, I feel like a miracle, a million dollars. I feel like pinching myself every single day. I'm just so grateful.

My childhood home was in a village in Nyeri County about two hours away from Nairobi, the capital of Kenya. I was twenty-three and in my third year at Nyeri Technical College studying secretarial services and business administration when my mom's friend referred me to a company for an internship in the city. I commuted via *matatu* (taxi) from my Auntie Frashier's apartment in Nairobi to my internship office. I had no idea that God was about to send me an angel. Her name was Agnes.

Agnes was a lovely lady, and since I was helping her with her work at the office, we became close. The objective of her project was to educate women about entrepreneurship and business. I was helping Agnes prepare for a seminar in America; we were coordinating with a nonprofit organization called Maendeleo Ya Wanawake. In May of 2000, the United States Congress approved the African Growth and Opportunity Act (AGOA), which intended to foster stronger trade relations between the United States and some African countries. Thankfully, a portion of the AGOA funds were used to support the Maendeleo Ya Wanawake organization's efforts, including my trip to the conference.

One day, Agnes asked me, "Would you like to go to America?"

I said, "Yes, absolutely, but I could never afford it."

Agnes asked, "Do you even have a passport?"

I said no.

She said that she could get the passport for me. "Do you have the money? It's two thousand and seven hundred Kenyan shillings."

That was a fortune for someone like me. Twenty-seven hundred Kenyan shillings was equivalent to about twenty-seven American dollars. I couldn't manage to pay for it. But I told Agnes, "You can go and get the passport, and I'll go ask my mom to give me the money before the two weeks are up." I gave her my birth certificate and everything she needed.

I was a student, and my mom was struggling to pay my college fees. I came home and asked her for twenty-seven hundred Kenyan shillings. She just said, "I'm so sorry. I don't have that kind of money."

I told her a white lie. "Don't worry about it, because this lady named Agnes has offered to pay everything for me."

I was still considered very young, in our culture, to travel abroad. My mom was afraid that I was not mature enough to go so far away. She also worried that I had college to finish. But I told Mom that I'd be back, and I'd finish school. Two days later, I had my passport, and Agnes told me we were going to America in two weeks!

Agnes informed me that I was required to attend a special meeting with the women's group at the Serena Hotel—a ritzy, classic hotel where only the elite or rich people go. Agnes advised me to dress the part and wear a traditional Kenyan outfit called a *kitenge*. She knew, however, that I didn't have the resources to pay for such a fancy dress, so she introduced me to her friend who worked above our offices.

Agnes's friend was a seamstress who sewed *kitenges*. Shortly after I arrived, the seamstress measured my body and stitched my dress. Before I knew it, I was trying on my outfit. The dressmaker even constructed a headscarf for me, since I couldn't afford to do my hair. To my surprise, Agnes paid for all of it.

During the meeting, I sat with prominent, well-educated businesswomen from the United States. I wanted to touch their skin and feel what it was like to be American. I was young and impressionable, and I admired the *muzungus* (Caucasian people) from the land of milk and honey. As I sat next to a woman who, in my eyes, was glowing, I felt like I was in the presence of a celebrity.

The speakers explained that when we arrived in Florida, they would teach us how to become businesswomen. Even during that time of my life, I was passionate about business, and I think that's why I'm the owner of a business right now.

All of a sudden, the speaker announced my name along with the other women who had visas to go to America. I was shocked. What was this? I didn't go to the embassy. I was not interviewed. Yet I now had a business visa to come to America with a group of wonderful women. All of the other recipients looked wealthy, and there I was with nothing. That just doesn't normally happen. Even when getting a Green Card, you have to go and pay and line up and book appointments. But my visa—a little miracle—was just handed to me with little effort from me at all.

The next challenge was the airline ticket. There was no way in a million years that my mom could afford the airline ticket. So, again, Agnes and the group paid for my flight. My mom didn't believe me. My cousins and relatives didn't believe me. Nobody believed that I was coming to America, with well-known women in business, and with practically all expenses paid.

My mom scrounged up whatever money she could find in the house and offered her whole life savings. Reluctant to take it from her, I wondered how I would ever be able to pay her back. But I took it with all the appreciation in the world, said a prayer, and was off!

As our plane was landing, I couldn't believe my eyes. I was sitting in the window seat, but I might as well have been in heaven. I saw the most beautiful green scenery I've ever seen in the world. I remember seeing a sign that read CHAI. *Chai* in my native language means tea, so I thought, *Oh, they speak Swahili here too?* I knew everyone spoke English, but just seeing that sign made me feel right at home. My heart was basking in happiness.

After Agnes and I retrieved our bags, we walked with the other women through the airport and outside. Everything I observed—the buildings, the roads, the grounds—was so clean. I was accustomed to rough, unpaved roads and dirt everywhere in Kenya. I had never seen such a clean environment as I now saw in Florida.

In Kenya, when I wanted to cross the road, I felt like I had to run for my life. There were few stop signs, and I rarely saw policemen directing traffic. Even the occasional traffic light was usually defective. So on August 13, 2001, when Agnes and I, pulling a couple of suitcases with all of our belonging, walked out of the Orlando airport and approached a crosswalk, I was stunned. The cars stopped for us!

At that moment, I felt free.

Men, driving all kinds of vehicles, gave us way. Their behavior amazed me because men in my past could be violent, especially to women. People in Kenya lived with so much hardship that they often looked serious, stressed, and maybe even angry.

But on that day, the ordinary act of walking in the fresh air was like heaven to me. The drivers were smiling, and I could not stop smiling either. It's crazy, I know, to think that a crosswalk represents freedom, but when you come from the life I did, even a simple crosswalk is a little miracle.

Our crowd of women followed each other into the Wyndham hotel. I stayed with Agnes because she was the only woman I really knew. The grounds were a gorgeous sight! I saw beautiful greenery and flowers. Everything, just everything, was breathtakingly green. It was exactly like I read about in the books. America looked like a piece of heaven.

We walked past the swimming pool and up to our hotel room. I put my belongings on one side; Agnes put hers on the other. Then we slept. My first night in America—such a sweet dream.

The next morning, we were invited to breakfast downstairs. I'd never seen anything like it! This is what people talk about when they talk about America. I remember it vividly. There was just so much food. I wished I could take a picture or tell people about the kind of life I was living before I came to America. And I wished I could tell the people in Kenya all that I was experiencing.

I saw a huge buffet of food spread throughout the dining room. Paradise. I had my choice of everything: sausages, eggs, fruits, juice, and even coffee. I had never seen a bowl of mixed fruits in my life. I had never seen grapes. I had never seen watermelon. I had never seen so many things that I tasted that day. And even though my family owned a coffee plantation, coffee was untouchable for us. Coffee was high class and only for the rich people. But here I was, in America, drinking a cup of coffee.

Of course, I couldn't eat it all. I wanted to, but there was just so much. I was shocked and heartbroken to realize that all the leftovers were thrown in the trash. We never trashed food in Kenya. So much food was wasted that day, and all I could think about was how much the people in my village would appreciate the leftovers. We were often hungry in Kenya.

After breakfast, we were directed to another room to start the conference, and the kindness continued. The staff continuously offered us water and napkins. They attentively asked how we were doing. Do you want this? Do you want that? Such service had never been presented to me prior to that day. Now, whenever I see a Wyndham hotel, I'm filled with emotion. I smile, and sweet memories come to mind.

I, a woman, was given a chance to be happy, to be received with love and affection and respect. That meant so much to me. I was overwhelmed with joy.

I saw a new life. I was given a cake with a cherry on top, and there was no way I could go back to the struggle I left at home in Kenya. So I decided to stay. I said to myself, *I'll work hard and become a blessing to everyone I left at home. I'll become someone that the community in America would not regret about. I am free. I can do whatever I want. I have all of this in front of me. And I'm not going to waste one minute of my time in America.*

CHAPTER THREE

OFFSPRINGS

WHILE HELPING WITH MY NEWBORN daughter in 2008, my mom learned that she needed emergency surgery. I took her to the emergency room, and the nurse told her to remove her eyeglasses, hearing aids, and dentures. I told the nurse that Mom didn't have hearing aids or dentures, so when my mother took the dentures out of her mouth, I immediately burst into laughter. I couldn't help it. She looked so funny without her teeth! Mom wasn't offended, though. She understood me, and despite the pain she was in, she flashed me a smile.

Later, when Mom told me the story about losing her front teeth while protecting her little girl—me—all the humor escaped the room. My dad had hit her so hard that he knocked her teeth out. That's the type of person my mom is: selfless, resilient, and protective. My hero.

My mom finished school in class seven. My grandmother, who was essentially a single mother by that time, couldn't afford to send my mom to her next class. In our culture, girls were not supposed to go to school, and my grandfather didn't care about investing in a woman's education. My mom didn't let her circumstances stop her, though. She educated herself and eventually became a secretary at an income tax company in Nairobi.

In those days (and some even now), men in Kenya didn't think women should be working. They believed that women should stay home and tend to their families. But over the years, women have become educated and are working in businesses and doing great things. My mom's mother, *cucu wa* Kibira, followed the original tradition. She stayed home and cooked for the kids and maintained the home while her husband worked. Thankfully, my grandfather still provided for his family even after they separated.

While she was working in Nairobi, my mom met my dad. They got married in 1970 and started trying to have children. I was their firstborn in 1977, and I became my mom's "egg." She did everything she could—for my safety and for my survival. There was no way her egg was going to break.

And that's why when I was a little girl, my mother gave up her front teeth for me—to protect me from my father. Although he never abused me, she didn't know what my father was capable of. A couple of years later, Mom gave birth to my twin sisters (Josephine and Grace); two years after that, she gave birth to my baby sister (Margaret, also known as Maggie). Mom worked the whole time, and at some point her youngest sister, Auntie Frashier, and her sister-in-law Auntie Jennifer took care of us in the city. They cooked for us, washed us, and played outside with us. She was very kind.

My mom's biggest fault, according to my dad, was that she could not give birth to a son. Funny how the woman was blamed for such circumstances, when biology tells us that the man's genes determine the sex of the baby. But that's how our culture thought back then, and that's why my dad abused and disowned my mother. Thankfully, education and access to technology have transformed the thinking, and women are not blamed as much for the lack of male children.

When I was in class three around 1985, we were living in Nairobi. My dad worked in the national hospital as an administrator. He drank every day, then came home and beat my mom. I was traumatized when I saw my parents fight, and I still suffer the repercussions today. My mom eventually grew weary of the abuse and considered relocating to the country away from my father. My aunties on my father's side of the family actually convinced Mom to move us to the family farm where my dad was born. My aunties were all married, and nobody was living in the house that my dad built when he was younger. So the house was rent- and mortgage-free, and although the farm needed care, it was an independent source of provision for our family.

Mom took my sisters and me and left my dad in the city. From that point on, my dad would visit maybe once a year. Some years he didn't visit at all. His absence didn't bother us, though. We no longer experienced the fear that pervaded our home when he was around.

Long after my parents' separation, I came across a letter my dad had written. He was a very good writer and wrote in English. In the letter, he referred to my sisters and me as *offsprings*. Not *daughters* or *girls*. Of all the words in the English language, we were his *offsprings*. The word stung. I remember telling my mom that I would work so hard that my dad would have no choice but to regard women as equal to men.

In our culture, polygamy was not uncommon. Even my mom's father married two wives. My grandmother was upset that my grandfather was committed to another woman, so she stayed away from him and raised their children essentially on her own. I know my dad had a few other women on the side, and although I don't think he married any of them, I know he helped conceive more children. I've never met my half brothers and sisters, but I know they exist.

Throughout my childhood, I heard my uncles discuss my father's girlfriends and their kids. One year, when I was in high school, I visited my father to request money that I thought he should contribute to help our family. It was my attempt at child support, I guess. I found my father with a woman and her child, who looked just like my father. I never informed my mother about my father's mistresses or children. I just knew how much it would hurt her, so I kept as much of the secret to myself as possible.

The farm was Mom's freedom. She was never more joyful than when she separated from my dad and moved to the village. I could tell she was at peace. We all were, actually. The fear of someone coming home and beating my mother evaporated, and we could finally relax.

Relaxing didn't mean Mom sat still. No, she became more vibrant, and farming became her passion. She loved it. She's very happy when she's on the farm, and when she isn't—like when she's visiting in America—she calls home to ask how the cow and the goats are doing.

The four of us girls and Mom lived in a small wooden house. It's still there in Nyeri. We lived there for the longest time. Later, after I came to America, I built my mom a new house attached to the same wooden home.

When you opened the door to our original timber house, there were three rooms: a large room that served as the living room, kitchen, and dining room; a room that served as my mother's bedroom and a storage closet; and a bedroom for my sisters and me. My mom's bedroom had a bed and a big, wooden bureau where my mom secured our valuable documents. I don't know how Mom slept in that bedroom. It was dark and depressing, occupied by huge sacks—potato sacks, bean sacks, and maize sacks—that Mom saved for us from the harvest. Those sacks contained the food we'd eat for the next few months.

Moving to the farm was such a good idea for our family. Mom would sell any food we could spare to people at her office or to our neighbors. Sometimes she'd trade food for help with activities at the farm or some other type of work she needed done around the house. So, because of the farm, we had just enough food; that was unusual in Kenya.

My mom was a good cook. The kitchen had three stones set in a triangle shape on the dirt floor with a fire in the middle. The stones and the fire were like a stove or oven, and we cooked everything on them. Mom makes extremely tasteful meals. She's known for making delicious African flatbread called chapati. Mom also makes great *pilau*, an Indian dish of rice and spices that we make quite a bit in Kenya. Though we loved her food, we could never have seconds—just one helping each. My mom would always say, "You've had enough."

Our home, like most in our village, didn't have electricity. We used little kerosene oil lamps, and we could only afford to light them in the evening when it was dark. Mom prepared our food, and we all dined together as a family. After making space between the pots on the kitchen table, we completed our homework together by lamplight. How that happened is just amazing to me!

Mom hung a few family pictures and a yearly calendar she brought home from work on the walls. I'll never understand why the timber walls were painted white. The dirt floors and the drips from the iron sheet roof gave my sisters and me all the mud we needed to "decorate" those white walls.

My sisters and I all slept in the same bedroom. My baby sister, Margaret, and I shared a single bed, while my twin inseparable sisters, Josephine and Grace, shared their own single bed. If it rained at night, we'd all get wet. There were so many holes in the roof! I just covered my head with the bedsheets, tried to sleep, and hung the sheets out to dry in the morning. The sunlight beaming through the timber slats served as my alarm clock. We used little pegs to hang our clothes on a piece of wire or a rope that stretched from one corner to the other—a makeshift closet, if you will. Some of our other clothes were stored in wooden boxes, and all of our personal property fit in our small bedroom.

My sisters tell me I used to trick them into doing everything for me. According to them, I'd say, "Hey, give me that. Can you pass that? Can you wash the dishes?" They say I bossed them around. Of course, I don't remember it that way. I always had good intentions.

We'd talk about everything at night in our room. We'd share stories. We'd fight over inconsequential things, maybe a blanket here and there. Twin beds are pretty small, especially as you grow older and bigger. Despite the constant and close contact, we loved each other then, and we still love each other dearly now. Even thousands of miles away, we communicate on a regular basis—usually weekly, sometimes daily.

Our toilet and shower room were outside, right next to the house. The toilet was a little room with tin walls and a deep hole. I can't even imagine how deep it was, because if someone fell in there, they would never get out. In Kenya, building a toilet is usually a complex and time-consuming project. You called a few men, and they built it for you over the course of a few days. On top of the hole, they added big sticks (like a grate) and left a little opening just to take care of the business.

Remarkably, the toilet never smelled bad. We tried to disinfect the area around the toilet with hot ash, and I guess because the rudimentary drain was so deep, you didn't notice any odor until it was almost full, which took years. When the toilet needed to be replaced, the men would come and cover the hole with soil. Then they'd plant maize and bananas on top and dig a different hole. The entire process was normal for me back then. When I compare that part of my life to my life now, though, I laugh. I'm amazed that my life is so different.

Toilet tissue was hard to come by in Kenya and was expensive. So we'd put some water on old newspapers and air-dry them a little until they became soft. My mom's generation used leaves. Most homes had a special tree that grew leaves with one soft side to be used for toileting. More people can buy toilet paper now. It's much more accessible, but when my mom was growing up, money didn't grow on trees—toilet paper did.

Our showers barely resembled those that I enjoy in America. The shower room was just a room with sticks on the dirt floor. We'd put water in a small metal or plastic bucket and splash it on ourselves. We didn't have soap, washcloths, or towels, but we did use strips of old clothes to wash ourselves.

We had what Kenyans call tap water. But again, tap water there was not the same concept as tap water in America. There was an enormous watering hole about a mile away from our house that would fill up when it rained. The reservoir had a tap, so we could easily get to the water without wading in it first. Every morning, we'd walk to the hole to get water for the day. When Mom had enough time before work and on most weekends, she would fill up her *mtungi*, a container that looked like a jug or a bucket, and tie it with a rope to her back. She'd also fill and carry two smaller buckets. My twin sisters and I carried a bucket in each hand; Margaret was too little to help back then. We had to transport enough water to last for a full day of drinking, cooking, cleaning, and bathing, or it was back to the tap. Once we got it home, Mom had to boil the water to kill the germs, especially if we planned to drink it. Procuring clean water was a time-consuming process.

It was very far, and I hated getting the water. Every time I'd use water, I'd think, *Oh, it's almost finished. Who's going to go get it?* Sometimes I even avoided taking showers or washing my clothes so that I didn't have to fetch it. Retrieving water and foraging for wood to cook with were the hardest chores.

Nowadays, people have concrete bathroom floors, and some even have the toilet inside their homes, but many families still live like we did in our old timber home. When I came to America, I sent my mom some money to renovate the original house. I made sure the wood was replaced. She added a concrete floor and painted. The house even has a sink now and a full bathroom.

Mom always put her daughters first. She was strong and resilient. She was able to work and continue to take care of four girls, even through the hardships she suffered. I see that as strength. Moving to my dad's family farm must have brought my mom emotional pain, but she unselfishly sacrificed for us. And, surprisingly, I think the farm was the best thing that could have happened to my mom and maybe even to us, her *daughters*.

CHAPTER FOUR

THE CHARCOAL IRON BOX

ONE DAY I OPENED THE LID, put a few hot charcoals in the hole, and waited about a minute or two until the iron box was warm enough. I poured water on Mom's work dress to prevent it from burning and started to smooth out the wrinkles. Not unexpectedly, a piece of charcoal fell on the dress. My mom was so upset with me when she saw the burn mark. She needed that outfit to look professional at her job. That was the nature of the charcoal iron box, though. If you didn't have a good one, then the hot coals ruined the clothes. If you were lucky, only an ash would land and dirty the garment. You'd start all over again, but at least the outfit wasn't ruined. That was an awful job. I didn't like ironing clothes for my mom, and I still don't like ironing clothes for myself.

Washing clothes was a big chore that we saved for Saturdays. First, we fetched the water, then we washed all of our clothes by hand, hanging them outside to dry with little pegs. Next, we washed all of the blankets, sheets, and towels. Dirt was everywhere, all the time. Thankfully, we did own beds, but the mattresses were paper thin and low to the ground, so everything was dusty or dirty.

In America, washing clothes is so much easier. I just throw a load of clothes into the washing machine, and when the cycle is complete, I transfer them to the dryer. No fetching water, no little pegs, and no dirt flying around. I can start a load anytime I want, and I don't even have to wash my own clothes if I take them to the dry cleaner.

Mom would buy me a few Sunday-best outfits because I was her firstborn, and she'd save money to buy my sisters and me two or three used outfits around Christmastime. We'd wear the same church clothes every Sunday. When we were not in school, we wore secondhand clothes that were sold on the stands (like a marketplace) in our village. They were hand-me-down clothes, but that's all we could afford. Of course, my sisters wore my hand-me-downs because they were younger than me. They used to say that Mom loved me more than she loved them because I got most things new — or, at least, new to us. You can imagine, though, that since clothes were expensive and took so long to wash, we didn't own many outfits.

On school mornings, my mom would heat some water and put it in a little bucket. We'd all wash our feet and brush our teeth. Then my sisters and I would put on our uniforms.

Around seven in the morning, we started walking to school. When my sisters were young, Mom would walk them to school before she left for her job in the city. We walked about three miles each way in our bare feet. I don't know why, but the chiggers loved my feet. So did the stones. Eventually, Mom was able to save enough money to buy us shoes. Shoes were a welcome addition to my wardrobe.

After school, we arrived home to an empty house. Since Mom worked in the city and I was the oldest, I took care of my siblings. At least, I was in charge until I was in class four, which is when I went to boarding school. While I was away, my mom had to depend on neighbors for childcare and light housework for a few hours each afternoon until she returned. That's just one more reason I find it surprising that my education was so high on my mom's priority list. My being away at school made life harder for my mom.

Weekly housework commenced with the impossible task of sweeping the mud floors. Then since our house was not equipped with electricity for heat or a stove, we'd fetch wood to build a fire. Sometimes we'd cook dinner before my mom arrived around five thirty or six o'clock. She worked about fifteen minutes away by *matatu*. We didn't own a personal car.

Our neighbor would come to milk the cow for us, and Mom would pay him with food or money. We made tea in the evening after dinner while we did our homework. My mom always reminded us that math wasn't her forte. So, when I was struggling with it, we'd invite our neighbors for dinner, share the little bit of food we had, and study together.

In addition to the cow, we had a few goats and chickens. Goat milk is so yummy. I loved goat milk, but we only had a small portion—just enough for us, none for sale. We didn't eat a lot of goat when I was a kid, but nowadays, we eat a lot of goat when I go home to Kenya. Mom has many running around, and it's normal for us to slaughter a goat. If a special visitor was coming over, we might have eaten one of our chickens. Most of our meals were meatless, so we looked forward to those dinners. We didn't consider most of our animals as pets; they were staples of our food supply.

My mom used to prepare the chicken on her own until I matured and wasn't afraid anymore. We'd start by boiling water—really boiling it well. Then we'd chase the chicken that we wanted around the coop, catch it, chop off its head, and remove as many feathers as we could. Of course, when we deposited the chicken in the boiled water, the remaining feathers would fly all over the kitchen. Next, we hung the chicken upside down for about an hour until all the blood drained out. We'd butcher the chicken into pieces, cook it like a stew, and dinner was served! Eventually, I was able to slaughter a chicken on my own in the blink of an eye.

Mom always stewed the chicken, so we could eat half of it one day and the other half the following day. Refrigeration, and even ice, were not part of our home yet, so we stored the food for the next meal in handmade clay pots. When the pot is cool, then the food will stay cool. When the clay is warm, then the food will stay warm. We didn't preserve or even cover our leftovers like we do in the States. In America, we store our leftovers in a clean container and stash them in the refrigerator overnight. I can only imagine what got in our food when I was a child!

When the cow gave birth, if the calf was female, my mom would try to sell the mother cow. We'd be left with the calf until it grew up and gave birth. If the next generation was a bull, we'd keep the Mama cow and sell the bull. We needed a way to sustain ourselves from year to year, and the female cows were a source of steady provision for us. My mom was (and is) so smart.

It's funny that we valued both genders of our cows more than some of our culture valued women at that time. My dad didn't think girls were worth much, and he treated my mother like she was a stone in his shoe. My parents separated when I was in class three, and we barely saw my father for the next sixteen years. Little did he know that my mom would raise us to be tough, independent women who didn't need his support anymore. She worked hard and sacrificed to educate us. She taught us to be grateful, to say please and to say thank you. She taught us ways of living as Christians and as ladies.

I spent a lot of time with my older cousin Jimmy. He owned a stand at the mini-shopping center in Nyeri—kind of like a farmers' market in America—where he sold secondhand clothes. Jimmy was like an angel to me.

Jimmy's mom and my dad were siblings, and he is about eight years older than I am. Every time I needed a little pocket money or I needed money for something small but essential that my mom couldn't afford, I'd go to Jimmy, "Please give me some money, Jimmy." He'd give me the funds to buy anything I needed. Jimmy was a blessing who never requested that I repay him. He often bought me lunch, like a loaf of bread and my favorite soda, a Coke. He treated me like his own sister.

Soda and bread were expensive, and my mom would only purchase them on special occasions, such as a birthday or maybe a payday at the end of the month. My mom encouraged us to eat beans and maize and potatoes from the farm so that we could save our money to spend on higher priorities. Bread and butter or even a kilogram of beef were rare privileges for us. You can see why my visits with Jimmy were a big deal for me.

One day in 2001, Jimmy accompanied me to the stage to hire a *matatu* back to my village. As we were walking toward the station, I saw a man sitting on top of his wooden suitcase. I said, "Jimmy, there's Mzee Mmoja," which was my dad's nickname.

Jimmy said, "What's he doing here? Where's he going?"

We hadn't seen him in many, many years. We approached my father together, and I tapped on Dad's shoulder. "Dad, what are you doing here?"

He looked up at me and said, "Shiru [my nickname], I'm coming home."

My dad had retired a year before. For some reason, he was not living with the other women and children who had occupied part of his life. And since the government no longer allowed him to reside in free or discounted housing, he had no choice but to go back to the home he built in the country—back to our three-room, wooden, iron-roof home on the farm.

During the ten-minute drive, my head was spinning. He's sitting on a suitcase. He has nothing else with him. I haven't seen him in years. He seems kinder than he did before. What's he doing here? God, please don't let him be violent towards my mom.

And I noticed that he would not let go of the suitcase. He just wouldn't let go.

My father was never violent with my sisters or me before he left, so I mostly feared for my mom's safety. When my father was growing up, it was normal for men to believe that they must beat their wives, or their wives would never submit to them. But girls turn into women over a sixteen-year period, and my dad was in for a big surprise.

When we entered the house, my mom was startled, then afraid. She welcomed him home with open arms, but from a distance. She wasn't sure what was going to happen next. She didn't overreact or become dramatic. My mom is truly a remarkable, humble person.

My sisters and I immediately met in our room. "What do we do?"

It's in our tradition to treat men in a certain way, like they're superior, basically. You're supposed to ask them if they want to eat. You wash their hands. You serve them. You soothe them. The whole nine yards. The prodigal son was back, but this time, instead of four scared girls with a single mom, he found five grown women who knew their worth. There was no way we'd let him take advantage of or mistreat our mom. Never again.

When I looked at him, I saw a man afraid to speak. A man who loved his money and his alcohol more than his own life. A man who was very sorry for what he'd done. And as the prodigal son's father forgave, at that moment I also forgave my father. I took pity on the sad man who didn't believe he deserved to be welcomed but had nowhere else to go.

He moved back in as if nothing had ever happened. In actuality, though, we were basically strangers to each other. Our conversations were filled with small talk, no chemistry at all. "Hi, how are you? How's everything? Would you like something to eat? What's going on in the city? What's in the news?" We were cautiously optimistic about him coming home.

A couple of months after Dad reappeared, I emigrated to America. My sister soon realized why he was so attached to the suitcase. His retirement money, his whole life savings—about a million Kenyan shillings (ten thousand American dollars)—were in that suitcase. He rose every morning, withdrew some money from the suitcase, purchased a newspaper, and resumed his drinking schedule at the local bar. He did that every day until the money was gone.

We called him Mzee Mmoja. *Mzee* means an old guy, and *Mmoja* means one and one and one and one. He was an old guy offering to buy beer for everyone in the pub. Yeah, he had his money, but Dad didn't share it with us. Most of the day, he sat in his chair and smoked—we hated that smoke smell. He wasn't violent. He was, if I may say, reserved, and maybe even a little depressed. And I think my independent sisters and I intimidated him.

My parents were like the charcoal iron box. My mom attempted to make my life as smooth as possible, but my dad had the ability to burn me if I wasn't careful. He was my father, and I respected him for his role in the family, but he didn't have influence in my life anymore. My mom did, and her influence uplifted me.

At that moment
I also forgave my
father.

CHAPTER FIVE

CREATE HAPPINESS

I LOVED WHEN IT RAINED IN KENYA. I'd go find a hilly place with my sisters and my friends. Then we'd carefully remove our dresses and stand there in our undershorts and little tops while we tied banana leaves together. We'd hop on our makeshift sleighs and slide down the mud like we were the Kenyan Olympic bobsled team. When the fun was over, I'd scrub away all traces of our secret recreation and venture home. Mom still doesn't know that we used to toboggan in Kenya!

Even when I was a little girl, I knew that I had all I needed to create my own happiness, my own heaven. I've always appreciated my blessings at each point in my life. Sometimes my blessing was just getting a meal in a day and hope for another meal tomorrow. Sometimes my blessing was the opportunity to go to school, learn something from the teacher, and (hopefully) avoid a beating. I'd assure myself that tomorrow would be an even better day. I grew up knowing that what I had was all I had, and what I had was more than I needed. It was enough, and I was okay with that.

Most American kids don't comprehend how hard it is for Kenyan or African kids to get the same things Americans already have. American kids can get a toy or an outfit or food right away. They can get in a car or hop on a bus and get to a store in a matter of minutes. Lots of American teenagers have jobs that allow them to make and spend their own money. Kenyan kids don't have the same opportunities. But I believe all kids, whether they live in America or Africa, should appreciate what they have, work hard, and create their own happiness.

For example, we didn't have toys when I was growing up. Toys were expensive, so we made our own. And I believe we had more fun than kids who have toys handed to them. My sisters and I played a keep-away game with our friends. First, we made a ball from leaves, wet newspapers, and the thin, plastic bags like the type Americans get in the produce section at the grocery store. Voila! The ball was hard, but it could bounce. Next, we'd spread out, and one of us was stuck in "the middle." The objective of the game was to keep the ball away from the player in the middle by throwing it over and around her. When she finally caught the ball, another player would take her place.

We'd also tie a thready plant to make our own long jump ropes. That was a lot of fun. We gambled a little bit too. We used to bet on the number of big seeds that fell from the trees. (That was when I was older and was able to obtain a coin here or there to bet with.) The player whose guess was closest to the number of seeds on the ground won the money.

My family didn't own a television before I came to America, and I was not a movie fan growing up. On Fridays and Saturdays, the owner of a big plantation used to host film viewings on an enormous screen. I participated because everyone else was going, but movies were not my favorite activity back then. Music was.

Listening to music on the radio was one of my passions. When I was a teenager and even when I was in college, I listened to hip-hop, reggae, and country music from America. I loved Baby Face, Boyz II Men, Mary J. Blige, Mariah Carey, and K-Ci & JoJo. Of course, who could forget Kenny Rogers and Dolly Parton? Country music was popular in Kenya and is trending up even now.

At an early age, I led younger kids from our village in Christmas caroling, and when I was a preteen, I joined a music group from our church. We gathered together with our instruments, practiced some music, went to tournaments, and won! Our version of Sunday school was full of worship and lively entertainment.

Although my mom is a good singer, I didn't get her gift of song. My strengths and passions were dancing and playing music. A *kayamba* is a flat instrument like a tray that has seeds inside. I'd shake it to produce a rhythmic sound, like a rattle that complemented the rest of the music. I played a home-made instrument that I made out of bottle caps. I used a stone to drill a hole in the center of each cap. Then I either put the caps in a tin can or tied them around my ankle. As I shook the caps, they'd make a lively sound that got people excited to dance and sing. And now that I'm in America, my kids love listening to me play a little drum that I place between my knees. Music has always brought me so much enjoyment!

When the British colonized Kenya, they brought Christianity along with them. Thus most Kenyans practice some form of religion. My grandmother raised my mom with strong values as a Presbyterian. On Wednesdays my grandmother led her children to church for prayer groups, and on Sundays they attended church services with their congregation. Church was an important part of my mom's life, and she made it an integral part of our lives.

We attended church every Sunday, participated in Sunday School, and sang or played with the choir. My mom always stepped up to volunteer, and when she brought us with her, we learned to serve through her example. Up to date, my mom is still very active within her church, and I am active in mine as well.

My mom's a prayerful person, and if I'm going through a lot, I call on her for advice and prayer. She'll tell me not to worry about my problem. God will take care of it; we'll pray for a resolution, and God will hear us. All we need to do is obey and have faith in Him. Immediately, I'm confident that good things are going to happen. And they do happen.

When I was nearly a teenager, one of the church elders spoke to us about what to expect during our adolescent years. In addition to explaining the physical changes of puberty, she counseled us. During the eighties, lots of girls got pregnant and dropped out of school or married at an early age. The woman from church advised us to keep our minds busy—as I remember it, she was trying to teach us how to not think about boys. Her abstinence guidance was not direct enough though, so my mom asked my auntie to educate me, specifically about preventing pregnancies. I was grateful for their concern. In the eighties, though, there was still that elephant in the room called HIV. Even though I saw so many people affected by HIV, nobody taught me how avoid getting the disease. Thankfully, my choices, influenced by my reverent fear of my mother and God, protected me.

Our parents were fearful that something bad would happen to us if we succumbed to the feelings that come with puberty, so they gave us the impression that dating was the worst crime a Kenyan teenager could commit. Many of my friends courted behind their moms' backs (truthfully, I did a little bit too), and they found themselves straying outside of their family's guidelines and values. The kids would have been better behaved if their parents had not prohibited them from dating. I choose to raise my children a little differently. I advise each of them along the way, "When you have a special friend, let me get to know your friend. Let me know what you're doing and be honest with me." I know my children, and I think having a dialogue with them is a healthier way to help them become responsible adults.

When I was about fourteen years old, I met the first boy who had a crush on me. I didn't want to break the rules and suffer the consequences, so I was hesitant to allow him to date me. Then one day, my auntie and his uncle got to talking. They realized we were spending romantic time together, and they confronted us. I thought we'd be in trouble for breaking the dating rule, but it was worse. They told us we were related! Of course, that relationship ended right there (admittedly, with a little laughter). My first boyfriend and I still talk quite a bit, but obviously, our connection never went anywhere.

In Kenya, we refer to our extended family as our clan. My clan has a lot of aunties and uncles, grandmas and grandpas, and (apparently) distant cousins. Although my mom and her siblings were very close, her only brother passed away a long time ago, and one of her sisters passed away during the birth of her child. Auntie Margaret, Auntie Frashier, and my mom are still close; they are sisters as well as friends. They visit with each other all the time, and they are always willing to help each other. When I was young, my aunties lived a distance away, however, so when we had a need, my mom often relied on our neighbors, who were also like family.

If I was sick and my mom had to work, a neighbor would care for me during the day. If one of the animals got out and was destroying plants on someone else's farm, our neighbors would come together to bring him back. And if we did something wrong, our elderly neighbors would discipline us. We depended on each other. It's become a cliché, but that's truly what it was like to be brought up by a village.

We spent holidays with our extended family. Easter was always a big deal. People would walk around with crosses and perform prayers. The Kenyan Independence Day was another holiday we celebrated together. We'd gather at one of my auntie's homes for a good meal. We didn't have fireworks like the American Independence Day. We didn't have television to watch. But we did have a radio to listen to the Kenyan president give his speech every year. The adults would discuss politics while my cousins and I played together. We topped off the day with a treat: a rare thirty-minute *matutu* ride home or an overnight stay with our cousins.

Christmastime was huge in our family. My mom had a specific idea of what she wanted a Christmas tree to look like. We usually searched until we found a citrus tree about two to three feet tall with a fresh smell to it. We'd place it on the kitchen table for a few weeks. Instead of ornaments, we decorated with cotton wool (similar to American cotton balls) that looked like snow on the tree. Then we placed all the cards my mom received from her work friends and our aunties on the branches.

Christmas is my favorite holiday now, and I definitely overdo everything! I send lots of ornaments and decorations to my family. And now they have enough room in the house to celebrate with a really tall tree. I just want everyone to be happy and enjoy the season.

On Christmas Eve, my mom would go shopping and buy the flour to make her special flatbread. We'd prepare a chicken to have meat for dinner, and we'd make a special meal before I took the village kids out Christmas caroling. On Christmas Day, we'd dress in our Sunday best clothes to go to church. We usually got a new outfit for Christmas, and much later in my childhood we even got new shoes. My mom had a passion for knitting, and she used her hobby to knit sweaters, socks, and even tablecloths for our family. After church, I'd make fried dough treats with the carolers, and we'd have a delightful dinner with our extended family, including most of my aunties. Christmas was a long, holy, festive day.

My Kenyan Christmas was very different from my American Christmas. In Kenya, we didn't exchange gifts; we didn't even know anything about presents for Christmas. We created our own happiness with what we did have—a simply decorated and beautifully scented tree, a bit of cotton wool, some music and games, a delicious meal, our family, and—of course—a whole lot of laughter.

CHAPTER SIX

LEARNING IN FEAR

THE WATER ON THE GRASS DIDN'T bother me too much on a normal day—but oh, those stones. The stones dug into my bare feet as I ran to school with my plastic bag of books and a pen. I was only in class one, but I knew if I was tardy, those stones would be the least of my problems.

I didn't want to go to school. It was too far from home. I had to walk or run by myself, so my mom could walk with my younger twin sisters. And when I arrived, I was greeted by teachers who were, first and foremost, disciplinarians. I was scared most of the time.

The local day school I attended from kindergarten through class three was not like the schools in America. I sat with seven to ten other students at a long wooden table set on the dirt floor. The room for classes four and above, at least, had a concrete floor, but none of the classrooms had electricity. A freestanding blackboard was at the front of the classroom. We sat in a dimly lit room trying to concentrate and learn until we were allowed to play outside for a little bit.

Sadly, the stones and the classroom environment were not the worst parts of my school day. The worst part was the discipline. If I didn't know something, I was spanked with a big, heavy stick on my back or the top of my hands. It didn't matter that the teacher hadn't taught me the lesson yet. The overwhelming message I learned was: Beat first, teach later. I would not wish my school experience on anyone. It was hard, and I was always struggling to create my own happiness in that building.

Thankfully, most of the modern Kenyan schools have changed quite a bit, and beatings are not as prevalent. I still see some social media videos of beatings in rural areas that are hard for me to watch. They are heartbreaking and evoke devastating feelings of anxiety. I think the leaders of the schools back then were not as knowledgeable about the way students learn. I'm grateful that my children have a more pleasant and effective educational experience led by instructors who teach a lot and don't beat at all.

When I was about to enter class four, I overheard a conversation between my mom and my uncle, who was a priest.

He said, "It's a nice school run by the nuns. The kids are well disciplined. Shiru is your firstborn and would be good at it. You should take her there so she can have the right education. Let the younger girls go to the day school, but give your firstborn the best education you can."

"It's too expensive. I can't afford it."

"Now that you have your government job, you can get a loan to educate her," he said.

My mom followed my uncle's advice. She applied for and received a loan from her employer, and she enrolled me in St. Teresa's Girls Primary School in Nyeri. St. Teresa's was (and still is) a well-performing boarding school for girls about twenty-five miles away from my village. I'd live at school for three terms per year, and my mom would pick me up after each term was over.

St. Teresa's was a modern, stone-built, Catholic school with electricity and well-cultivated flowering gardens. People were cleaning the school all the time. We lived in long dormitories arranged by grade. The bathrooms were nicer than at home, and they were attached to the side of the school. The science laboratories and agricultural equipment were much better than the tools we could use in the rural schools.

The nuns led the school and were tough disciplinarians— just one of the reasons why the girls performed so well. Like the teachers from my local school, the nuns arranged all the students who failed an exam into a line, plucked a hard stick from a tree, and beat the top of our hands. Some days they might use a ruler instead of a stick, but either instrument was intended to induce maximum pain. I tried so hard not to fail an exam. I studied even when the other kids were sleeping until I could get it right. I lived and learned in fear.

Since it was a boarding school, we also ate together. For breakfast, we ate plain porridge cooked in big pots. Truthfully, all meals the school served were cooked in big pots. It was tasteless prison food, but there still wasn't enough to fill my belly. My friends and I were always hungry, so we'd hide raw maize (corn) and rice in the bushes to eat during the week. We weren't allowed to bring food to the dormitories. Looking back on it, I don't know how we ate raw maize and rice, but we were starving. Anything was better than nothing.

The lack of food and the frequent beatings made me miss my family. I couldn't call home, so I usually cried and cried until I could console myself. As time went on, I made some lifelong friends. Despite the beatings and the hunger, we had a lot of fun in school. There was time to play and time to read. We liked to knit and sew together and talk about where we came from. I loved hearing my classmates' stories. We enjoyed watching and participating in performance groups and music groups.

Some of my friends from boarding school actually live in America now. My friend Carol lives in Boston, Massachusetts. Mary is in Washington, D.C., and Miriam actually lives in Lowell, Massachusetts. I catch up with all of them and more on social media. And I'm pleased to say that they're all doing well.

Many of the families of the kids who attended school with me were well off financially. I was one of the kids that were kind of on the poor side. The elite families owned cars, so on each semester's Visiting Day, the parents were at the school early. I spent much of Visiting Day sitting in a corner crying and afraid that nobody would come to see me.

When my family arrived later in the evening, I was so relieved. My mom had a tougher life than most of my friends' parents. She had to cook food for me all morning; gather up my little sisters; and, unlike most of the other parents, she had to hire two *matutus* just to arrive in time for dinner with me. Mom found a way to bring everything I wanted—bread, meat, cookies, soda—and since we didn't have refrigeration, she had to make all of it right before they came to visit. I was extremely happy that I got to see my family on those visiting days.

At St. Teresa's, thirty to forty students were in each class. We all had our own desks and our own books. The teachers were elevated on a narrow platform, and the blackboard was attached to the wall so we all could see. We were allowed to speak only English at school. I did well in English grammar, and reading was my passion. I was proficient in social studies and home science, but I was often beaten because I wasn't an accomplished mathematics or science student.

I went to high school at Mary Immaculate Girls' Academy, another prestigious Catholic school. And when I passed all of my high school exams, I decided to go to Nyeri Technical

College (Nyeri Tech) to study secretarial services and business administration.

Nyeri Tech was closer to our village. I still had to take a *matutu*, but the overall cost was less expensive than the cost of other Kenyan colleges. I adored my college education. I had always dreamed of working in a bank, because people who worked in banks in Kenya had unique privileges. They were paid well, and they had access to more opportunities. From the time I was little, I had so many things I wanted to do businesswise, and Nyeri Tech was the perfect place for me to start working toward those dreams.

My mom once told me that the only thing she could provide to benefit my future was education. She said, "I can't afford to buy you clothes. I can't afford to take you out and have fun at restaurants, but I can provide education to you. I want you to work hard at it, because that's what I think will help you in the future."

My mom was only allowed to complete class seven. She knew exactly how much education would mean for me as a girl growing up in Kenya. My mom squeezed her budget and sacrificed relaxation and pleasure to make sure that I would be educated well. I am the person I am today because of my mom and my sisters. I owe it all to them. I didn't finish Nyeri Technical College, but I accomplished so much more than I ever dreamed I could.

CHAPTER SEVEN

I WOULD BE DEAD

IF I HAD NOT COME TO AMERICA when I did, I truly believe that I would be dead. I know that sounds harsh, but I
believe it's true. The Kenyan lifestyle at that time was turbu-
lent, especially for girls. Nobody cared. Girls were grabbed
and raped, and nobody would talk about it or even think that
was an offense. One time I was going to school, and a man
grabbed my breast. I was so offended and humiliated that I
thought I was going to die. As the men stood around me and
laughed, I felt stuck. Alone. No one was willing to help me.
Even if I had reported it, nothing would have been done. It
was normal for such things to happen. If I had stayed in
Kenya, I would not have survived.

Domestic violence was normal when I was growing up.
Stealing was normal. General violence was normal. People
couldn't fulfill their basic needs, so they turned to crime just

to put food on their tables or roofs over their heads. They'd grab whatever you had—from supplies to your body to your self-respect—and no one in authority would attempt to stop them.

Sometimes my mom would struggle to get a full plate of food on the table—but we had the farm, so there was always something to eat, even if it was the same meal I had yesterday. Sometimes I would get sick, and Mom would give me over-the-counter medicines instead of a more expensive hospital visit. Sometimes I would see the people around me who were extremely poor dying in their homes with no one to help them.

So when I landed in America and saw people offering the crosswalk for me to pass freely, it was kind of like healing. I was here, and I couldn't believe it. I knew I was going to achieve the American Dream.

As much as I tried to work hard in school to be a good student, I didn't think it was possible for me to be who I wanted to be in Kenya. In Kenya, you had to be rich and know someone with influence to get into certain universities or hired for certain jobs. My mom did the best she could, but every month she divided her paycheck into basic needs— food, school, clothing, and some medical checkups. The other things were just not able to be a priority for us.

Mom worked hard to bless me with a better education, and I knew she struggled financially. When I was in high school, I needed money for fees and other supplies, so I decided to visit my father and persuade him to contribute toward my expenses. I didn't tell my mother, but I did tell my twin sisters. They looked forward to my coming back and sharing the funds my father supplied.

I was named after my father's mother, my grandmother Nancy Wanjiru Kamenju. We shared the same first and middle names; Wanjiru is the origin of my nickname, Shiru. The generational connection between my grandmother and me unexpectedly created a stronger bond between my father and me. Because he thought of his mother when we were together, Dad was more generous with me than he was with anyone else. The trick, however, was that I could not imply the money I requested was intended for anyone else's benefit. If he thought the money was for something I needed like shoes or books or supplies, then he'd eventually relent and open his wallet. But if he thought I'd give the money to my mother or my sisters, he'd refuse to help. I learned his game, and I started taking a *matutu* to request my informal child support payments about twice a year.

As a young girl, I had to muster up all my courage to travel to my father's offices in Nairobi and Embu, both dangerous cities. I'd use a little bit of pocket money to pay for the *matutu* and arrive at his workplace very early in the morning. On the ride over, I'd remind myself of my "why"—why I was willing to take this risk: I was going to see him to give my mom a break. I didn't like lying to my mom, and I didn't like being afraid to approach my dad. I was his child, and he should have taken care of me. I reminded myself that I was just making the trip to survive, and he owed us. He was our father, after all.

I'd track him down, and he'd tell me, "Let's go outside." We'd leave the building, and I'd explain why I needed another installment. He'd smoke and pace, smoke and pace. Then he'd buy us lunch at a little restaurant, and he'd drink. He was a tough man to talk to, so we didn't talk in much detail during our meal. He'd ask me surface questions like, "How's your education going? How are your grades?"

My father was intimidating, and since he was drinking, the whole experience was even more terrifying. When I asked him for the money, part of him wanted to give me the money, and part of him didn't even want to see me. He was so agitated and unpredictable. He was the type of man who'd suddenly snap and slam his fist on the table. I'd recoil and shout, "Oh my God." I was terrified that he'd hit me. I was afraid the whole time I was with him.

We never talked about his life or his other families. A few times, I discovered him at his home instead of at his office. That's when I confirmed he was living with another family—the other woman and their kids, my half brothers and sisters. Even though he knew I happened upon his secret, my father never spoke of his other family to me, and I never spoke of them to my mom or my sisters. I didn't want my loved ones to hurt like I was hurting.

Once we completed our transaction, I'd hire a *matutu* home. Sometimes I'd give a portion of the payment to my mom. If she asked where I got the money, I had to lie. I'd tell her my friend gave it to me, or my auntie in a nearby village gave it to me, or my cousin Jimmy gave it to me. Most of the time, I used the money to purchase school supplies or to pay school fees without her knowledge. I shared whatever I had left with my sisters for pocket money. Every little bit helped.

My mom raised me to be a good Christian girl. I knew I wasn't supposed to lie, so I was tormented by the sin of those visits and my actions when I got home. I had to weigh the situation, though, and helping my mom financially while saving her from heartache was critical to me.

I'm glad I took those risks, because those risks made taking other risks, like trusting Agnes, easier. After the women's business seminar in Florida, Agnes disappeared. I can't even remember what she looked like or guess where she is right now. There was no Facebook then. We didn't take any pictures. We didn't exchange any contact information. I have no connection with Agnes at all. If I saw her face today, I would not recognize her; yet she was the angel sent to me by God. She was the one sent to bring little miracles to my life.

When the conference ended, Agnes and I parted ways. My mother had arranged for me to visit with my auntie who lived in Massachusetts, so I headed for the airport.

In the air I was thinking, *How blessed am I to be here? I'm going to work so hard. I'm going to be the best that I can be in this*

country, and I'm going to help the people in my village back home.
A few hours later, I was waiting in Boston's Logan Airport,
but I could not find my auntie. I waited and waited and could
not connect with her by phone. So I called my cousin, who
also lived in the area. He arranged for our long-time Kenyan
family friend to pick me up and take me to her house.

When the family friend arrived at the airport, someone
else was also in the car. During the drive I could sense that
something was just not right, yet I was too excited to realize
that I might have been inconveniencing my new hosts. They
weren't expecting me, and I quickly learned that our friend
was planning to move across the country two weeks later. I
begged my cousin to come and get me, but he was not available. I had no other place to go. I was stranded, alone, in
America. So I stayed with our friend for a few days until my
cousin could bring me to his family's home. I am extremely
grateful to all of them for rescuing me during my time of
need, for unexpectedly taking me in, and for assisting me as
I settled in this country.

My auntie was my dad's first cousin, and I knew her very
well. Growing up, I regularly played with my cousin. Naturally, since they were family and we were close, I was more
comfortable staying with them than I was imposing on a
family friend. They lived in Lowell in a two-bedroom apartment. David, my cousin's friend, was a frequent visitor.
David and I became friends.

On September 11, 2001, I was sitting in the apartment, watching the news report about a plane hitting a building. I didn't know what was happening, so I continued watching while my heart pounded in my chest. A few minutes later, another plane hit another building. *Was the building right next to me or somewhere else in Lowell?* I tried to call my cousin, but he didn't pick up his phone. What else could I do? I called the only other man I knew in America. I called David.

"David, what's going on? Where are those buildings?"

David tried to calm me down. He said, "America is getting attacked, but the buildings are in New York, about four hours away from us."

He knew I was distraught, so when he finished his work shift, he took me out for lunch. He had no idea how hungry I was. My auntie had been so gracious to let me stay with her family, and I didn't want to be a bother. I had not asked about food before they left the apartment, and even if I had asked, I hadn't learned how to cook using an American, modern stove!

My first date with David was at the McDonald's on Bridge Street in Lowell. By the time we got to the restaurant, I was famished. I had never eaten a burger before—certainly not one as juicy and huge as a McDonald's burger. My life had changed forever.

Communicating with my mom and my sisters back then was a challenge. I had a grandfather in my extended family who lived about a mile away from my house in Kenya. He was a businessman and doing very well financially. His house had electricity and a phone, so when I needed to get in touch with my mom, I would call his house. By the time my message got to my mom, the whole village knew that I was doing okay.

The day I called to tell my mom I wasn't coming back home I knew she was scared. She pleaded with my aunt to protect me. She reminded me that my visa was only for five years and advised me to come home. I wanted to spare her feelings, so I told her that I would return in six months. By the next time we talked, she had become used to my departure, and she had calmed down. I assured Mom that I was very happy, but I didn't tell her about David or that I was living with him.

By then, I knew that my life had potential. I had escaped what I considered certain death. I had been given a few more little miracles: a loving family to live with; my boyfriend, David; and a juicy McDonald's burger. Life couldn't get any better than this!

CHAPTER EIGHT

I BOUGHT MYSELF

IN AUGUST OF 2001, I MET A MAN. By September of 2001, we were good friends. By December of 2001, we knew we were in love.

In January of 2002, David was rooming with four men, and he asked me if I wanted to move in with them too. I went from living in a house with five women to living in a house with a bunch of men and their girlfriends. My mother would not have approved, but I was in love with a man who was trying to uplift me. He was trying to show me the way in America, and I liked that quality in him.

You might think that I'd be afraid of getting close to a Kenyan man. After all, I had only recently left a culture of violence and abuse of women. But I trusted David because of the man he was. To tell you the truth, I was not afraid at all. I felt free.

Freedom gave me the courage and the confidence to trust. I loved America so much, and most educated Kenyan men here were different. Maybe it's because in America there is enough for everyone. In Kenya, everybody wants something from someone. Men, especially, wanted to steal your personal belongings and your happiness. I guess it goes back to not having hope. They just took.

But David was different. He didn't say, "Hey, let's go. I'm dating you. Be my girlfriend." He didn't physically or verbally try to hurt me. He didn't put me down. He lifted me up through a prolonged friendship. He listened to me. He was respectful, and so were his friends. They gave me the space I needed. They were friendly. And when David was around, we'd all talk and laugh and share stories. It was a completely different relationship with men than I was used to back home. David was my protector, my friend, and the love of my life.

We lived right near the Council on Aging in Lowell, off Broadway Street. It was a nice house, but it could get messy. I'd get up in the morning and clean and clean and clean, then cook. The other girls were busy with work, but I wasn't allowed to work in America yet, so I took care of the domestic responsibilities for everyone. Most of the guys ended up marrying the girls, and we all remained friends. I especially enjoyed weekends. We'd order pizza and watch football together. That's why I love football now. The guys taught me all about it.

At that time, David worked in group homes and a computer company. Most of his group home clients, especially those in the state-run group home, were mentally challenged teens. Later, he worked with older adults with Down's syndrome. He lived at the home for a few nights each week. He assisted clients with their medications, made sure his clients were safe, and also did some direct care like washing, bathing, cooking, and laundry.

Later in our marriage, David left the computer company and took a job in the information technology (IT) department at a pharmaceutical company in Cambridge, Massachusetts. He eventually transferred to an office nearby in Waltham. During those years, he'd work his overnights at the group home from eleven at night until nine in the morning. He'd come home and start his IT job from eleven in the morning until five every night. With the exception of a few years, David worked two jobs on very little sleep to support us.

Dating David was pretty amazing. I had learned to enjoy movies, so we often went to the Crosspoint movie theater. Shopping was my hobby. David would give me money, and I'd go to the Ames department store down the street. I think they all knew me at Ames because I was there every week, shopping for kitchen stuff and clothes. David spoiled me.

We enjoyed getting away from everything for a little while. We traveled to the White Mountains in New Hampshire and visited Maine and Texas. Most of our vacations were spent on or near Cape Cod in Massachusetts. We'd rent a house for a week in Falmouth, Yarmouth, or Hyannis and invite our friends for the weekend. Sometimes we'd get a hotel room, but usually we stayed in a home where we could also entertain.

We had so much fun together. The beach was David's happy place. His peace. He'd sleep on the sand the whole day. After a few hours, I'd be back in the room reading or maybe taking a walk. Later, we'd come back together and talk and just dream.

David's dream was to work for himself on his own schedule. That was my dream for him too. About three years before he passed away, David quit both of his jobs and achieved that dream.

One of my dreams when I first came to America was to own a car. We didn't own cars in Kenya. We had to hire *matutus* to drive us from one place to another, or we walked. After I learned how to drive, David took me to a car auction in New Hampshire. I spied a beautiful, maroon Dodge. The inside and the outside were spotless, and I liked it. David said the most important part of a car was the engine, but regardless of the engine's potential defects, I wanted my Dodge anyway. David raised his hand to bid, and we got the car for five hundred dollars. Thankfully, the bid was within his price range. We brought the car home, got it repaired, and used it for many, many years until it broke down.

I used to go over to Shedd Park in Lowell near the fountain and watch people driving their cars. I wanted a Nissan Altima so badly that when I saw one I'd say a prayer and tell God that I wanted the car that just passed by. So when the Dodge broke, David bought me a used Nissan Altima that I drove for a few years.

David had his car dreams too. He wished he could drive a Mercedes. In 2014, when David was going through more cancer treatments, I bought him a preowned, gray Mercedes. I had saved up enough money, and I wanted to make one of his dreams come true. He loved it.

David was always good to me. One day in 2002, we were sitting in the living room of our new apartment on Park Avenue in Lowell. He turned to me and asked, "Would you like to marry me?"

I looked at him and laughed. Then he took out a ring, and I asked, "What are you doing?"

"Would you like to marry me?" he repeated. "I know you don't like surprises, but this is just between you and me. I got this ring from Walmart."

I said, "Yes," and hugged him.

It's the best ring ever, because it's what he could afford back then. It has never chipped or anything. The color is still the same. I thought his admission was so unique because he had studied me. He knew the real me. He knew that I liked simple things and no surprises. It was a special and lovely moment between the two of us, exactly the way I would have liked it.

A couple of years later, David and I told our parents that we were engaged and wanted to do a customary marriage. I remember my mom saying, "Are you okay? Is this a nice guy? I don't know him." I assured her that David was a gentleman, but since this was before the age of smart phones, I could not send pictures or anything.

In Kenya, you're not allowed to live together before marriage, so I didn't tell my mom. When you want to marry, you go to your parents and tell them that you've met a man you love. They inform the elders. Announcing your intention is the first part of the process.

Then the man is expected to pay a dowry—usually cows and goats and money—to his bride's parents, relatives, and close friends as gifts in appreciation for bringing up their daughter. It's like the man is buying the woman, and I don't like it at all. But it is tradition, and our families expected us to follow our traditions. We agreed.

Since we were enjoying America's economic blessings, the whole dowry became very complicated. David and I were from the Kikuyu tribe, which is in the central part of Kenya. There are forty-two tribes in Kenya, and each has its own traditions and cultural expectations. Normally, the village elders assess how you were brought up and the class of your family to determine the amount of dowry that must be paid. For example, if the bride went to a boarding school and her father owns a certain amount of land and a house, then the dowry might be set at a million Kenyan shillings (about ten thousand American dollars). Someone else might have grown up in a family that doesn't have much and her class is lower, so the dowry is set at one hundred thousand Kenyan shillings (about one thousand American dollars).

In our case, since we had the potential to make more money than either of our families, we (not the elders) decided what my dowry amount should be. Then David and I worked for years until we could pay it. That's right: I bought myself.

We chose two hundred thousand Kenyan shillings, which was very low, considering that we were living in the land of milk and honey. That's what we could afford, but some of the villagers were disappointed. They wanted more. We didn't have more. In their defense, they didn't know what was really occurring in our lives at that time. During those five years, I was educating my sisters back home, trying to live a stable life in America, and paying for David's cancer treatments. No one knew David and I were working really, really hard to save that money.

There was another issue to resolve. According to our tribe's tradition, if my mom's dowry was not paid before David and I married, my mom's relatives and our marriage might be cursed. Back when my parents were engaged, my father started but never finished paying the dowry to my mom's family. Even though I had announced my intent to marry, my father refused to fulfill his responsibilities. So my hero bought herself, just as I did.

Mom bought a cow and a bull and gave them to her oldest nephew, her eldest brother's eldest son. If my father had paid the dowry before they married, then the cow and bull would have been given to my grandparents. If they had already passed, then the dowry would have been given to Mom's eldest brother. By the time we announced our intent to marry, they were all long gone. The dowry rules are weird by American standards, but it's our tradition, and we respected the customs of our heritage.

A payment of a cow and a bull was just one more sacrifice my mom made for me. Her dowry cleared the path for David and me to marry. By 2006, we had raised enough money to go back and present my dowry to my mother and our village. David was too sick to travel, so I went alone. I told everyone that he was working and couldn't get vacation time to join us. David sent the dowry money to his parents, and I went to the ceremony in my Dress Barn sparkly top, a black skirt, and black and white shoes.

Fifty to sixty people came to witness the exchange of the dowry. We slaughtered a few goats for the village to eat and for the blessing. Then the elderly men drank goat blood and Tusker Kenyan beer, while most of the women drank soda. The elders poured some of the goat blood on the ground and said a traditional prayer to bless us. David's family showered my family with lots of gifts—maize, beans, flour, sugar, rice—

as a thank you for raising me and allowing me to marry their son.

My mom received a significant allocation of the payment. My uncles and aunties, the tribe elders, and the villagers each received a portion of the remaining money so they could bless me.

The paying of the dowry meant we were married by traditional Kikuyu standards, but we still wanted to be married in America someday. In March of 2013, my mom was visiting to help out after our son's birth. David and I woke up one morning and had the shortest conversation of our lives.

David said, "Let's get married." It was from out of nowhere.

We had no plans. We just walked into Lowell City Hall and got married. David and me. That was it. It was that simple. We didn't even bring my mom with us, but we did invite the justice of the peace back to our home to perform a repeat ceremony in front of my mom and our children, Nikki and Jesse. David told me that he didn't think we needed to announce our marriage to the whole world, provided that we loved each other. I agreed, but I still wanted a big wedding like the American weddings I had attended. David always tried to indulge me, so he said, "In 2014, you're going to walk down the aisle at St. Michael's church."

But when 2014 came around, David's cancer was acting up. I was starting the business, and we were working out our finances. The church wedding would never happen.

Left to right: The justice of the peace, my mom,
David, Nikki, Jesse, and me

CHAPTER NINE

SO WE DANCED

WE HAD A LITTLE RADIO that we played outside our house. When I was still a kid—maybe from the time I was eight to fifteen years of age—I'd gather twenty to thirty other kids from our village and encourage them to dance. Then I'd give them candy. Somehow I was able to scrape together a few coins—less than an American quarter—to buy some candy. I always tried to keep a little pocket money around, and if I didn't have my own, I'd "borrow" it from my sister Josephine.

Josephine organized all of her belongings—clothes, school supplies, money—in our tiny bedroom. If she owned even one penny, she knew exactly where it was. We each had a small metal box where we put some of our clothes. Inside the metal box there was sort of a metal pocket. Josephine would tie her coins in a napkin cloth and stuff the coins into the hidden compartment. She was smart. Nobody would have thought her savings were there, but I found them. I'd take some of the coins and buy candy—sometimes for me, sometimes to reward the children in our village for dancing. But Josephine never found out that I was the one who "borrowed" her money until we were adults.

Eventually, some of the kids would just come and dance for me on their own. They knew I'd find a reward for them. Those kids are adults now, and many of them still call me. They say, "Remember how we used to dance at your house?" I had so much fun back home.

On Christmas Eve, I'd gather the children together to sing Christmas carols from America. We'd practice at our compound, then perform from house to house. People would even pay us! We'd get the equivalent of an American dollar from each family and buy flour. My mom and my home science teachers taught me to cook well, so we'd use the flour to make fried dough to celebrate on Christmas Day. My mom would say, "Why are you taking my oil? You need to buy your own oil from the money you make from singing." I think I made her broke a little bit, but we all looked forward to that fried dough.

Home science was a class in primary school where we learned how to sew clothes and bake. I loved baking. Outside our home, the kids and I made a fire using charcoal and firewood. Once the coals were hot, we'd set a large pot on top and pour buckets of sand inside. We nestled the batter-filled cake pan in the warm sand that slowly baked the cake for us. Then all the kids and I ate dessert.

When I came to America, there wasn't much work I could do until I had the right documents. So I would make food like my mom taught me and sell it at the African Festival in Lowell. I was the first Kenyan to manage a stand for the festival, and I was even featured in a story in the newspaper! I cooked a special dish we call *githeri*, a mixture of maize and beans. Mom's *githeri* always tasted better than mine. She was also known for her flatbread, which had soft, thin layers of skin coming off of it. When I make it, the bread is hard. (Mom hasn't shared her secret with me yet.) For the African Festival I'd also make big trays of *pilau*.

Since I wasn't allowed to get a real job yet, I did a lot of babysitting. I was introduced to a Kenyan pastor and his wife, who needed a babysitter for their three children. One time, the pastor sent his friend, an older pastor (I'll call him Pastor Z), to pick me up for that day's babysitting. I had a cold and asked to stop for some medicine. Pastor Z helped me buy an over-the-counter cold medicine and told me to drink it right away. I was young and naïve and didn't know that the medicine was only for nighttime. I quickly became drowsy.

He drove me to his house, put a movie with naked people in it on the television, and started to touch me inappropriately. I screamed and ran around the house to escape the molestation. It became clear that he was going to try to rape me, so I fought him. I pushed him and ran, screaming at the top of my lungs, out of his house. I walked all the way from his house back to the pastor and his wife's house. I was numb.

I told them what had happened, but they didn't believe me. I cried myself to sleep that night. David wanted to go to the police, but I didn't think anyone would believe me. That's how it was in Kenya, and that's how it was with the pastor and his wife. How could I trust that things would be different if I told Americans?

About five years later, I ran into the pastor and his wife again. They apologized for not believing me. Pastor Z had since been deported because he was abusing his wife. I was able to forgive all of them, but I regret not going to the police earlier.

I also cleaned houses for people. Cleaning houses was a humbling experience because in Kenya, only rich people hired housekeepers. I pictured myself as a house helper back home, and it was humiliating. But I did it, and I usually got a hundred dollars for cleaning somebody's house, which is much more than some house helpers are paid in Kenya.

I was so driven to make myself useful as an American and to support my family back home that I would do just about anything legal, and within reason, to earn money. When I went to parties, I'd collect bottles and return them to the store to recoup the deposit money. I could earn about five cents per bottle, maybe twenty American dollars for one party. I'd divide the twenty dollars and send ten dollars home to my family so they could eat.

I was a proficient bottle collector, but again, it was humiliating. When someone in Kenya collects bottles, that person is assumed to be poor and homeless. Even though in Kenya collecting bottles is something I would never do, I focused on what I was going to get from the American bottles. I knew if I sent ten dollars back home, I could feed a lot of people. And that's why I did it. I didn't look dirty or roam the streets. I just went to happy places and helped my friends clean up after the party for a small reward equal to the bottle deposit.

David guided me through American life, from going to school to getting a job to becoming a citizen. The only thing he didn't do was teach me to drive. Our friends taught me to drive because David and I would always argue in the car. At that time, we were living with four of his friends who owned cars. Another good friend, Geraldine (I call her G.) patiently taught me to drive. Macharia, one of our friends, also taught me to drive. I was grateful that everyone was willing to let me borrow their cars, but I could only choose from the two that were not manually operated stick shifts!

When David and I started dating, he worked in a group home and thought I would also be a good caretaker. He suggested that I go to school to become a certified nursing assistant (CNA), so I could work in one of the nursing homes or assisted livings. He even paid for the class for me. A month later, I became a CNA. I was really good at taking care of people, which was a blessing because we never expected that our lives were about to change drastically.

In 2004, David and I had recently moved to Park Avenue Apartments, and we were ready to start a new chapter together—without housemates. One morning I noticed that David had a swollen lump right behind his ear. I asked him, "Do you have mumps?" He went to the mirror to look at himself. "There's something swollen by your ear," I said.

But he was just like a typical man. He said, "It's nothing. I'm not in pain. It will go away."

A few months went by and the lump remained, so we scheduled an appointment to see his primary care physician (PCP). I could see the doctor's reaction just from the mere touch of the lump. "Have you been checked? Do you smoke? Does anyone in your family have the mumps? Has anyone in your family had cancer? Have you ever had anything like this before?"

He referred us to another doctor for a biopsy. Right before we went in for the procedure, David looked afraid. I sat down next to him, and I told him, "I'll be here, and we'll fight this together, no matter the outcome."

A few days later, we went back to his PCP's office for the results. Cancer. "You have six months to live. But with a good lifestyle, you can live longer. You need to exercise, eat well, avoid stress, and just be a happy man."

I was terrified. I didn't know much about cancer. I thought it was the end of everything, but I didn't tell David that. I thought, *David's gone. I don't think I'll have a husband or kids or even a wedding.* Feeling afraid, I incessantly researched the disease, its symptoms, and potential treatments.

We started practicing living "clean." I'd buy organic foods at the grocery store or the farmers' market. We'd exercise together at the gym or in our basement, and we'd go on vacations. Every minute mattered.

David stopped smoking. When we met, I saw David smoking once and told him how much I hated it, so I didn't see him smoke very often; he smoked mostly when he was around his friends. But after he learned he had cancer, he gave up smoking right away.

David started chemotherapy (chemo) and radiation treatments at our local hospital. We were thankful for David's friend Bernard who drove David to some chemo sessions. Eventually, his doctors referred David to a better hospital in Boston for a clinical trial of a new chemo medication. The cancer cells began to shrink.

Every week, a nurse came to check on David's chemo port and put another dose of medication through. The chemo session would take six weeks, then a couple of months later the hospital would take the port out. The chemo would make David really, really sick, but after the session he'd regain his strength. And that's what our life was like—for ten years. Every few months he'd go back for a test, the cells would be growing, and he'd get another round of chemo.

The cancer was in remission from 2015 to 2018. During that time David was very healthy. His blood pressure was perfect. He was eating well. I started my own home care business. Life was good. Then in July of 2018, David got pneumonia and was admitted to the hospital in Boston, where his doctors discovered that the cancer had spread. This time, they prescribed a higher dose of chemo and radiation for six weeks. For the next round, they told him to take chemo as a pill instead of through the port. That worked okay, but I could tell his body was becoming weaker and weaker. Everything had changed.

We started spending more time together. I made sure that David was happy and lived a full life. That was my "why" for starting my business. I wanted my husband to have the option to work from home or not work at all. After working for the pharmaceutical company for more than a decade, David turned in his resignation letter. Soon, he left his job at the group home. When he was feeling well enough, David worked with me on the business.

The cancer spread to David's nasal passages. He had trouble breathing, which kept me awake, so the doctor prescribed a nightly medication. In October of 2018, the cancer spread to his brain. That was really rock bottom for him. The news drained him of his spirit of hope and his potential to survive the disease. He stopped doing a lot of things. He would look at our kids and cry. Still, no one in our circle of family and friends knew that David was sick. He just didn't want to talk about it.

Around May of 2019, I found out David had been hiding his prognosis from me. His doctor didn't think David would live until December, and David agreed. I don't know how long my husband lived with his secret, but I know he was trying not to hurt or scare me.

"I hope you're prepared. I hope you will be able to take care of the kids and the business. I don't think I'll be here," he said, "I just feel very weak." I assured him I would. He couldn't even go upstairs by himself. I would guide him up the stairs and help him dress. When he couldn't put on his own socks, I knew he was in bad shape. He just had so much pain.

On June 21, a Friday morning, David said he was going to work from home. I could tell he was in pain, but every other time he had taken his pain medication, he went right back to normal. When I came home from work, the kids had supper and went to bed.

David and I sat at our little kitchen table and had fun talking and drinking until early morning. We talked about the house we were just about to buy in a nearby community. We called a friend of his from Seattle around midnight our time. We laughed and reminisced a little more. David took his breathing treatments. Then a song from Kenya came on the TV, and David said, "Let's dance."

So we danced.

We'll fight this
together, no matter
the outcome.

CHAPTER TEN

AMERICANS

Most people who were born as Americans have no idea how blessed they are. I've seen many of them underutilize the resources they have here and underappreciate their freedom. If I had had everything that Americans have when I was born, I would have conquered the world—or at least cared for a few more elderly residents and Kenyan families.

When I came here, I wanted everything America had to offer. Within a couple of months, I found the man of my dreams. Even though he got sick, we wanted an American family with a couple of kids. We had so much love to share, and we wanted all of us to experience the American Dream.

When David was first diagnosed with cancer, the doctors told him he had only six months to live. Then they said one year. Then another year passed. And as the years flew by, David appeared to become stronger. We both believed in a higher power who knew better than we or the doctors did.

And we believed that if we continued to do the right things while David took the right medications at the right times, he could beat the cancer. We had so much hope.

Eventually, we stopped listening to the predictions that the doctors gave us, and we lived our lives as best we could. In 2005, I told David that we were going to have a baby. He was bursting with joy! Three and a half months later, I had a miscarriage. I think I was more affected than David was, because I had already told a few people. I was so prepared to have our baby, and the feelings of loss were overwhelming.

I had been working double shifts at the assisted living facility, and I started to wonder whether it was my body or David's cancer that caused the miscarriage. So I scheduled a visit with David's doctor. He was helpful, but nobody, not even he, knew why the miscarriage happened. I was so sad, but we were willing to keep trying to grow our family.

After we moved to our Lundberg Street townhouse, I got pregnant again, and this time I got to see the baby's ultrasound. He was a boy. When he was twenty-six weeks in my womb, I had a perfect checkup with my obstetrician. By nighttime, I was feeling uncomfortable. Then my water broke, and I was having so much pain. I told David that we had to rush to the hospital. We went to our local hospital, and the nurses told me I was actually giving birth. When I delivered the baby, he was stillborn. I glimpsed at his lifeless body for only a second. David and I were devastated.

When the doctors can't tell you why miscarriages are happening, you want to have hope. David's doctors weren't sure if the chemo and medications were affecting our babies, so we kept trying until we suffered through a third loss. By then we had endured enough heartbreak. We accepted that we might be moving too fast to grow our family, so we decided to take a break. My friend Carmala encouraged me during the hard times. We didn't share our pain with many people, though, and keeping the secret only added to our feelings of isolation.

Everybody kept pushing me. "Why do you have such a big house? You don't have any babies. Why are you wasting time?" But they didn't know our stories. Most people didn't know about the miscarriages or David's illness. We decided to wait until David was free from the chemo medication for at least two or three years.

One day in 2008, when David had just come home from working overnight at the group home, I felt a little weird. I went to the drug store, bought a pregnancy test, and told David to come upstairs and look at it with me. "Let me know what you think." He had no words. He was so overcome that he started crying. We were pregnant again.

This time, David treated me like an egg, just like my mom did when I was born. He treated me so well. He just wanted me and the baby to be safe, and he was so excited to become a father.

He pestered me, "What do you want me to do with the room?"

I said, "David, it's not even a month yet!"

He would hold me and try to convince me not to go to work. "Don't do anything. Just sit and sleep. Whatever you want. Whatever you need. I'll provide."

So I worked very little—about four hours a day—and at seven months I stopped working completely. We had a huge baby shower with all our friends and family at our house. Everyone was so thrilled, and it was just a beautiful day. Once our little Nicole—who we called Nikki—was born, Daddy and daughter played like two kids. David loved Nikki with all his heart and mind until the day he died.

When Nikki was two and a half years old, we got the happiest surprise of our lives! I started feeling morning sickness, and I told David that I thought I was pregnant. We bought a test kit, and sure enough, I *was* pregnant. Another baby blessing was unexpected but so loved already. In early 2012, I gave birth to a baby boy. We named him Jesse, and David loved him unconditionally and completely. Jesse was a very happy baby and is a happy child.

Over the years, I have seen and learned that God works in His own ways. He granted us two healthy children at just the right time. When I got pregnant with Nikki, David was in remission, and everything was fine. When I got pregnant with Jesse, David was feeling ill again and back on his chemo treatments, but I successfully gave birth to our second child.

David's illness taught me that I needed to trust God and His timing. His illness also taught me to be strong for my family. David was always upbeat and pushing me to do the right thing for our kids. I promised him that I would.

I'm glad that we did not get discouraged and lose hope, because we ended up with two beautiful children. The losses were difficult to deal with, but I knew they happened for a reason. Cancer is a beast. We fought the beast, and we won for a long time. We won long enough to build a family. Cancer tried to put us down, but we believed in God. We prayed a lot. We did the right things—all the things the doctors told us to do. We had to change the way were living. We had to eat clean and exercise. We had to give up alcohol and smoking. And we had to enjoy our lives. That's how we beat the beast for a long time.

Not only did I give birth to two miracle babies, but I gave birth to two Americans.

When I left Kenya, I needed a visa to come to the United States. That visa was good for five years. If I wanted to stay longer (and I most definitely wanted to stay), then I needed to get a Green Card. In 2004, David helped me hire a lawyer from Chelmsford.

I had to be a good person who obeyed all the rules, regulations, and laws. I had to file taxes and work. I couldn't come to America and expect to be helped by or receive funding from the government. I had to volunteer. Every step was a way of pushing me further to become a better person than I already was. I received a Green Card that was good for ten years.

The process to become a naturalized citizen—an American—was complex, lengthy, expensive, and personal. We had to save a lot of money to file the application, pay the lawyer fees, and attend interviews.

Then I had to study for the citizenship test. I read a United States history book that the agency gave applicants to prepare for the exam. I also had to speak English; fortunately, I already knew how to speak and read English. If I couldn't correctly answer most of the questions on the test, or if I couldn't speak English well enough, my application would have been denied.

Our lawyer also told us to practice the national anthem. That was a funny homework assignment! David and I would sing one verse of "The Star-Spangled Banner," get to the middle, and mess everything up. Thankfully, singing was not part of my test.

On a nice summer day in 2009, I stood in a big courthouse by the water in Boston and took the Oath of Allegiance to become a United States citizen. My mom, Nikki, David, and our lawyer came with me for this special occasion.

After all the officials were introduced and all the speeches were made, I stood and swore my oath to the United States. Then the other new citizens and I sang the national anthem together. The minute I saw the lady put the stamp on my certificate and the officials shook my hand, I looked at my lawyer and screamed, "Oh my God! Thank you, God! I'm going to use this to be the best American citizen I can be!" I told him, "I'm going to make you proud. I'm going to be a good citizen." I cried tears of joy. Yeah, I loved it. I was finally and officially an American.

Becoming an American meant freedom—a different kind of freedom than just being *in* America, as I had been for the previous eight years. Becoming an American brought peace of mind and comfort. It meant the world to me. I still tell myself what my lawyer told me throughout the process: America is for the brave and the fearless.

I was so proud to be a Kenyan and to be considered an American as well. I knew I could use my Kenyan-American dual citizenship to help hundreds of people around me and back in Kenya. And I have. I've been able to feed and clothe and care for so many people because I go out there fearlessly, earn what I can, and share it with others.

I tell my kids all the time, "You have everything. You have to use what you have as an American in a good way. No human, especially an American, is limited in what they can do. You must go beyond all perceived limitations." Becoming an American is why I'm able to be who I am now, and I'm so appreciative of the opportunity.

America is

for the

brave and fearless.

CHAPTER ELEVEN

LET GO AND FORGIVE

IF YOU DIRECT KINDNESS and compassion toward anything that's negative, the result will always be something
positive and loving. Many, many years before I came to
America, I was harassed by cruel, callous men I didn't even
know, and I never felt like I could report the offenses to the
authorities. It took me a long time to learn how to speak up
for myself and not feel like a victim.

My father, unfortunately, was a product of our culture's
misogynistic thinking. So when he came home for his retirement, our house of women didn't know what to think or
what to say. And although we were afraid, we knew that we
needed to be kind and loving toward our father while still
honoring our worth as women.

Our house was small and had only two bedrooms. My parents had to sleep in the same room, but Mom never

complained. She dutifully accommodated him—you're my husband, you're still my husband, you're still the father of my kids. She treated him with respect. She provided everything he needed, and he got up every day, went drinking, and spent all of his money on himself, his bar buddies, and women.

In December of 2006, I built my family a new house attached to my childhood home in our Kenyan village. It has three bedrooms (each with its own wardrobe), a living room, a dining room, a bathroom, and a kitchen. The huge refrigerator in the kitchen made the chances of spoiled meals and food-borne illness distant memories. My family can take hot showers inside the house and sit on a real toilet. When I was younger and we used the hole outside, I was so cold. I made sure that the new, large toilet room and shower room were heated. Now it's nice and warm for my mom and my sisters. Sometimes our neighbors come over just to use the bathroom, and the neighborhood kids love visiting our house.

One of the finest additions to the home was a separate bedroom for my father. He could come and go as he pleased, while my mother enjoyed the privacy of her own bedroom. My father always smoked and was often drunk. He coughed a lot and was definitely ill, but it took a while before we learned he had throat cancer. His bedroom served as a respite when he was feeling sick. He lived with my mom and my sisters for about ten years after I moved to America.

As the years flew by, my sisters kept me informed about the status of my father's health. I knew his cancer was getting worse. I sent acetaminophen and ibuprofen to help alleviate his pain. When I called to talk with him, I could tell he was losing his hearing, so I sent hearing aids. I'd even send him clothes and money for food. At this point in his life (and mine), I simply wanted to make him happy.

Miss Laura, my teacher when I attended school to become a CNA, and I had a very good connection. I remember she said, "You're going to go far, because you like this work so much. Why don't you become a registered nurse?" I got all As in her class, and I enjoyed studying. I couldn't afford an advanced degree to become an RN, though, and after seeing where I am today, I'm glad I didn't pursue a medical track. Home care and business management are my passions.

In April of 2011, I took Nikki home to Kenya to stay with my family and me for a month. By then, my CNA certification and experience rendered me a caregiving professional. I went to the hospital every morning to check on my father. He looked awful, and the doctors told me that he would die soon.

Towards the end of his life, my father became a good man. He was remorseful. He told me how much he loved my mom, my sisters, and me. He was very thankful. He told me that he was proud of me for all I had done for our family: building them a house, educating my sisters, facilitating a life that was better than even some men could (or would) provide. I proved to him that I was not just an offspring. I was an equal. During our last visit, he called me his lovely *daughter*, and I said goodbye. Before I even arrived at our farm, he had passed away.

Nikki and I were supposed to fly home that night, so I changed our flight and stayed for two more weeks. Kenyan funeral homes are not like those in America. They don't care for the deceased's body well or quickly; therefore, I relied on all my training to attend to my father even after he died.

I went to the funeral home, put on my gloves, and cleaned his body to prepare it for burial. I put cotton wool in his mouth and ears so the odor of death wouldn't seep out as much. Before I left America, I bought my dad a handsome suit. I dressed his expired body, and even though his weight loss made the ensemble appear oversized, he still looked stately. I wanted to do the right thing. He was still my dad. And no one else in my family knew how to ready a body for a casket, so I took the lead. I was grateful for some of my uncles and the funeral home workers who assisted me.

We held a traditional Kenyan funeral for him. People came for prayers every night for twelve nights. On the day of the funeral, friends and family cooked a buffet of food and supplied drinks for a few grave diggers who excavated a hole right next to our house for my father's grave. There was music. Then the pastors and priests arrived. After a short service, they lowered my father's body into his final resting place and buried him. We all honored and remembered my dad with a mercy meal after the funeral.

Forgiveness sets you free. My dad did so many awful things to me and to my family, but I learned to let go. Now if someone does something wrong to me, I speak up, and then I let it all go. And that strategy allows me to forgive the person. Forgiveness is not easy, but it does bring peace. I'll tell you if you've done something wrong to me. I'll move on, and our relationship will continue and grow. Unexpectedly, I learned that lesson through my ever-changing relationship with my father. I count that lesson as an invaluable blessing, a miracle.

Nikki and I returned to America to find that my salaried job at an assisted living facility in Acton was no longer available. I had been employed by the same company since the end of 2003. The manager told me, "We're not firing you. You can work per diem [on a per-day rate]." The organization was transforming, and the new leadership didn't know me well enough to advocate for my continued employment.

I had worked at the assisted living for nine years doing the work that I love: talking to the elderly, taking care of them, and listening to their stories. I had also taken a course to get my manicurist license. I didn't know anything about manicuring or other spa services, but I knew how much I loved taking care of my Grandma's feet when I was a little girl. My goal, at the time, was to give the seniors in the assisted livings the pampering they deserved.

While I loved caring for the residents and working with my coworkers and bosses, I hated being overworked and not being able to give the residents what they needed. I loathed watching them suffer, but as a CNA I couldn't do much to alleviate their pain. I wasn't a manager, or even a supervisor, in the company.

Some residents didn't like their food, although I thought it was pleasant. Some residents were just angry that they had lost their independence. And some residents didn't like the color of my skin or people who looked like me. My mom taught me that I must receive people the way that they are without judging them. When I met an elderly person who needed care but didn't seem to like me, I tried to be as kind and professional as I could be in their home or wherever I met them. Most of the time, before I left, they would embrace me with love. I don't know why I had that effect on people, but almost all of my experiences resulted in a positive fare-well.

If being kind and professional didn't work, I'd think of my client as an innocent baby or consider how the person was raised. How did their circumstances influence them to be the person they were that day? I'd sit back and just imagine that person being different—nicer, calmer, happier—at an earlier age. Even if the person was being unkind and abusive or try-ing to do things to hurt me, I would keep trying to show them that there's another side of me. There's something they might not have known about me.

Infrequently, I'd have someone who just wasn't ready to see the real me. Sometimes I'd speak up for myself once or twice. But if the client became violent or started calling me names in a loud voice, I knew it was best to step back—to let go and move on. I learned to prevent the memory of an ugly experience from permeating my heart. It's better to let go, forgive, and hope for something better.

I often worked with residents or clients who had dementia, a disease that affects the patient's whole family. I understood that the client in front of me was not who the caregiver's mother or father really was, and I could see and feel their pain. I went through lots of training, and I realized that the disease wasn't going to change for the better.

I remained calm and patient. If they told me the pen was moving, then yeah, the pen was moving. If they insulted me or verbally disrespected me, then I'd quietly say, "I'm sorry, I'm not [whatever the insult was]." And I'd continue to work without making a big deal about the comment. Controlling my emotions as well as immediately letting go and forgiving usually worked.

I was good at my job, but it wasn't just a job. It was my passion. David had endured my complaining long enough. He knew I wanted to take care of just one person at a time, and he knew I had an affinity for business. So when I returned home from burying my father, I worked per diem for a while, then called a few of my former supervisors. They agreed to send me contacts for private home care jobs. My dream of going out on my own and starting my business had begun.

He called me

his lovely

daughter.

CHAPTER TWELVE

I AM HUMBLE HOME CARE

I ALWAYS GO INTO MY CLIENTS' homes smiling and laughing. They say, "What are you so happy about?" And I say, "I'm just glad I'm here." Then we start the stories.

The secret to my business success has been absolutely loving what I do and completely believing in myself. The work feels effortless to me.

In late 2013, I went to a Kenyan party in a nearby town. At the time, I had been working on my own for more than two years. I met a man who said he helped people start their own businesses. I came home to David and told him that I was going to start the home care agency. For years, I had shared my ideas and plans and dream about the agency with my husband, but I was almost too afraid to believe that it could happen. That day, I told him I was going to register the business so that I could take care of more elderly clients. He laughed and said, "How are you going to do that?" But I knew I'd find a way.

The business consultant educated me about entrepreneurship in America: where to register the business, how to prospect for clients, how to file taxes, and all that. He connected me with the right people for insurance and workers' compensation. Because I was starting as a sole proprietor without employees, I didn't incur a lot of expenses. In June of 2014, I only had fifteen hundred dollars, yet I was a proud new owner of a business.

I needed a name for my company. When I looked back on my life, I realized there was one consistent theme: I was humbled by and grateful for so many miracles in my life. I was humbled by the fact that I came to this country, by the people I met in the assisted livings, by my father's illness and his change of heart before he died. I was humbled by David's illness and by the fact that God gave us two children at just the right time of our lives. I was so grateful to be in America, and that's why I chose such a simple name for my agency: Humble Home Care Services.

As people referred clients to me, I became too busy to care for each client the way I wanted to care for them, so I hired another person. I needed to figure out how to develop an application to hire CNAs, RNs who could supervise the CNAs and advise families, and even a marketing director. David was proficient with computers, so he helped me draft the application, paperwork, and contracts. As of the time of this writing, about five years since the agency has been in business, we've hired more than three hundred CNAs. We currently have about forty CNAs active on our payroll, and almost all of our clients come from word of mouth.

We take care of people who need companionship and nonmedical assistance. We help with bathing and showering, cleaning, cooking, clothes laundering, housekeeping, doctors' appointments, and even exercise. But when it comes to activities like taking a client's blood pressure or dressing a wound, we leave those services to visiting nurses from other agencies. The RNs on staff generally help advise our clients and their families.

My approach is always from the heart. I compare myself to and empathize with my current client and my client's loved one. I almost want to become my client at that moment, and I want to provide the best care I can for my client at all times. That's why my approach is different from most large corporations that provide care for the elderly.

When someone comes into the office to apply for a job, I meet with the applicant, and I tell him or her my story—where I came from and how I got to this point in my life. I tell them that I think of the elderly as my grandparents. I see my female clients as the neighborhood women whose feet I washed on Sundays in Kenya. I look forward to them sharing their stories with me. "How are you doing today? Where were you born? How many brothers and sisters did you have? What did you do in life? How many times were you married?" These are the types of conversations I had with my clients. All of their stories were unique, and almost all were funny. They made my day, and I had so much fun. I want the CNAs who work with me to follow my example.

I say, "This is what I want you to do. Can you do it?" I talk to each and every employee, so there are no misunderstandings. My example is my high standard, and there's no room for negotiation. My employees must know that it's what they do out of their hearts that makes the client happy. I want my clients to know without any doubt that I'm not just a random corporation or agency or franchise.

I *am* Humble Home Care Services. I am Nancy, and this is what I believe in.

Every week I visit a few clients. Whoever I don't visit, I call. Mostly, I ask, "Are we doing everything okay? Is there anything we can rectify?" Then they tell me the positives and negatives of our service, and I try to address any of their concerns.

And my method is working. There have been times when my business has flourished to the point that I've referred new clients to other agencies. I've also referred CNAs to other agencies when I didn't have enough clients to support a larger staff. I know that what God has put aside for me is mine, and that reward isn't going anywhere. And I know in my heart that God gives me what I can manage and nothing more. In Kenya we say: You can only bite and swallow so much.

Your tongue is very powerful. Whatever you say may actually happen. I used to tell my work colleagues that I was going to open my own assisted living organization, and I would care for patients better than we could care for them in the typical facility. My work friends always remind me that my words essentially came true.

I see lots of miracles every day. When I get a call from a client and they say everything is fine, that's a miracle to me. When I get a call to take care of a client, even if it's only for one hour, that's a miracle to me. When an aide goes to work and reports on time and does her own job exceptionally well, that's a miracle. When I get up in the morning and everything is flowing as it's supposed to be, that's a miracle. Being able to connect with so many people, to drive to a meeting, to talk to a client, to understand each other well, and to work as a team are miracles to me. Those little miracles—the connections and my love of caregiving—are the reasons I've been as successful as I have been so far.

Although I appreciated all of life's little miracles, secretly I prayed for another miracle. My real reason for starting my business was David. Way back in my head, I knew I was going to build my business so my husband could enjoy the rest of his life. I had to be brave and take risks, but those risks paid off when David was able to start working for Humble Home Care Services.

*I was humbled by
and grateful for
so many miracles
in my life.*

CHAPTER THIRTEEN

LIFE IS LIFE

DAVID HAD COME TO AMERICA in 1998 as an international electrical engineering student of Middlesex Community College. Over the years, he became an integral member of his community. A kind, loving, religious Catholic, David was one of the first few people to form the Kenyan Catholic Community at St. Michael's Church in Lowell. He also helped organize the men in Lowell and the Boston area to form the Christian Men's Association (CMA). They met, probably once a month, to talk and attend seminars about faith. As the chairman of the Kenyan Catholic Community for a few years, David had the opportunity to influence a lot of Kenyan men, friends, and family.

In 2018, David's illness forced him to drop his CMA responsibility, but no one from the group knew what was actually going on. They watched his physical body change, yet his mind and his attitude remained upbeat and encouraging. People from his church approached me so many times asking if David was okay, but David wouldn't let me say anything about his illness. Although he refused to say he was sick, they knew something wasn't right.

We lived with David's sister, Purity, in our house for a year and a half, and even she didn't know how poor David's health was. If she knew, then she was so respectful of our privacy that she never mentioned our secret. He'd get sick. His doctor would admit him to the hospital, and Purity would not know where we were. She just carried on and helped us with our kids and our home.

David was so private about the cancer and his treatment that it hurt me sometimes. He didn't want to tell me the whole truth. He just didn't want to be a bother to anybody.

Though David was sick for more than a decade, I asked our Kenyan families to start praying for him only a couple of years before he passed. Our nuclear families knew he had cancer, but they didn't know the details. I just said, "He's sick, but he's not going to die tomorrow. Please, keep him in your prayers."

We never knew when tomorrow would be *the* tomorrow, though.

After David and I danced in our living room that Friday night in June, I went to bed and left him with my cousin Erick, who had just moved to America and was living with us until he could get settled on his own. When they were ready for bed, David couldn't go upstairs. He was afraid that he would lose his breath, so I came down to the kitchen and gave him another treatment of his respiratory medication.

I wanted to call 911, but David didn't want to go to the hospital. The treatment worked well enough for me to help him upstairs. He slept until around five in the morning, when he shot up in bed, saying, "I can't breathe."

Panicked, I remembered that he was ready for another treatment. I kept telling him, "We need to call 911. Let's go to the hospital." But he just said, "No. I feel better. I'll be fine."

Around seven, I told Erick that I'd never seen David like this. We agreed to call 911, and the first responders arrived around seven thirty to take David to our local hospital. I requested that they airlift David to the hospital in Boston, but the doctors had examined him thoroughly enough to know that he was failing. He was stabilized in the intensive care unit (ICU).

On Sunday I asked the gentle nurse in the ICU if it would be okay for our kids to come to visit David. She said yes and assured me they could come for the whole day. David was sitting up in his chair from about eleven o'clock until five thirty. He was talking. He was jovial. In fact, he was doing so well that his nurse said she thought he'd be transferred to the regular ward the next day.

David talked with Nikki about school. Then he reenacted the *Uncle Drew* movie they had watched together the previous week. Dressed in only a light-green hospital johnny, he

starting dancing around the room with his new dance partner—another johnny. It made everyone laugh and helped me
forget about how serious the day was, at least for a minute or
two.

We tried to distract ourselves by talking about our up-
coming trip to Kenya. What did we need to do? How did we
need to prepare? I didn't think traveling was a good idea, but
they all argued with me. "No, we need to go! Daddy says we
should go!"

In the afternoon, Jesse was sleeping on the bed in the hospital room, and David kept tickling him. He'd say, "You know
I love you so much." Over and over he repeated those seven
words to both of our kids. It was such a memorable day for
me, but Nikki and Jesse didn't really know how sick their father was.

Purity picked Nikki and Jesse up from the hospital around
six thirty that evening and brought them home to stay with
Erick. By nine o'clock, David was doing okay, and I was so
exhausted that I said goodbye for the night. Erick decided to
return to the hospital and stay until David could fall asleep.
Erick and Purity were miracles for us—and still are for me.
They saw the struggles we had, and they jumped right in to
help with the business, with babysitting, with chores at
home—anything I needed them to do, really. I thank God for
them.

David was extremely uncomfortable until about two in
the morning, when the medical staff started giving him

morphine every four hours. His breathing was distressed. When I arrived at the ICU around six on Monday morning, his nurse told me that David had had an awful night. Maybe he was putting on a brave face when I got to his room; he looked peaceful and happy to me. We talked for a few hours about how he was going to rebound and come home. David thought he'd be strong enough to grill some goat meat, his favorite.

Since we had not gone to church on Sunday, there were a few messages on David's phone. I asked him if he wanted me to call his priest to join us for prayer and a visit. With a little coaxing from Purity, David agreed.

The priest entered the hospital room with another priest. David and his two visitors were all friends. The priests said a mass, blessed David with oil, and left. I asked David if I could call my pastor, and he agreed. My pastor and a friend spent a few minutes with us and said a prayer as well.

At that point, David didn't look as weary as he must have been feeling. I know the discomfort was a burden for him, though. Anybody in his situation would have been afraid and in agony. I couldn't do anything but comfort him. Unfortunately, my comfort wasn't enough. He required that pain medication just to survive. David looked right into my eyes and said, "If anything happens, take care of the kids, and I'll see you again in Heaven. I love you."

About an hour after everyone left, David took a turn for the worse. His oxygen level started to go down. His blood pressure was down. The room filled with nurses and doctors, and suddenly everything turned the other way around. I was in the room with him the whole time until he went into cardiac arrest and the medical staff tried to revive him. I couldn't watch. I felt a gut-wrenching helplessness. Those few minutes were filled with the most painful events I've ever experienced in my life, so I stepped out of the room.

And an hour after the priests' and pastor's blessings, my husband, my partner, my best friend was gone.

I couldn't believe it. I was devastated. I was numb.

Then as if a switch turned on, I went from no one knowing that David was sick for fourteen years to everyone knowing that he died. I'm not sure I was ready for that much attention at that exact point in my life, but I didn't have a choice. I had to explain everything that had happened over the past two decades.

David and I talked a lot about his wishes for himself and our family. Sometimes when Kenyans pass away, their bodies are sent back to Kenya for burial, but David made it clear that he wanted to be buried in America.

My mom and David's mom were able to get visas to come for the funeral. A couple of my aunties and a couple of uncles also came from Kenya. Unfortunately, my sisters were not able to attend.

When Kenyans pass away, friends and family visit to pray every evening for at least a week. Our small house with little parking was crazy and always full. People parked all around the main street and the side streets. The neighbors asked lots of questions. Even the police came to our house on a daily basis to see if everything was okay. People came in the hundreds. Thank God it was summertime! People sat outside under a tent and inside on the first floor and the basement. People were everywhere for all twelve days.

St. Michael's church was packed. Five or six priests who gathered from different towns around Boston led a Catholic Mass in Swahili. And, throughout the whole process, the people at Bailey's Funeral Home were so good to us.

David was buried right here in Lowell in the Westlawn II Cemetery; I call it the Boston Road cemetery. We had a short ceremony there and a mercy meal at the VFW Hall. David's friends and family talked and ate and said hi to everyone. Then we came home. My relatives from Kenya stayed for a few more days.

Months later, people still called and visited to check on us. It's a way of living as Kenyans. It's a very kind gesture that never ends, if I may say that. They popped in and out any day and any time, but mostly on the weekends. It's a tradition that can be overwhelming when you're grieving, especially if you want to protect yourself from some of the difficult memories—the illness and the last few days and the funeral. Yeah, sometimes it was overwhelming. But I appreciated the support more than they'll ever know. I'm grateful that so many people checked in on my kids and me.

I want Nikki and Jesse to remember the love that was displayed during the mourning period and on the day of the funeral. Hundreds of people came and talked and viewed David and gave speeches about love. Most people from the Kenyan community said David was the type of person every man looked up to. Nikki and Jesse should never forget that their father was a loving, giving, respectful gentleman.

David also wanted happiness and joy for his kids and me and for his family back home in Kenya. Nikki had her dad for only ten years, and Jesse had his dad for only seven. I know what it's like to not have a dad. And when you have a dad who is good to you and loves you and is willing to lie on the floor and wrestle with you until Mom yells down from the upstairs to keep all the racket down, ten years and seven years are just too short.

So David asked me to always remind our kids about him. The first time I was pregnant, I bought a book of baby names and went through the whole list. I wanted to name our daughter Violet. But since I was off and on sleeping after the delivery, I just agreed with David's suggestion of Nicole. Nicole was a common name on television at the time, and he loved the name. "I think your name sounds better," I said in a daze.

The same thing happened with Jesse. I wanted to name our son Michael, but David said that Michael was too common. While we were in the hospital, David said that he wanted to name the baby Jesse. He identified with the biblical story of David and Jesse. That meant Jesse was in, and Michael was out.

Our children began their special relationships with David on the days that they were born. David was a loving father. He wanted his children to have the world. He was a very playful dad, even up to the day he died. He gave them everything.

He was protective of the world they would live in even after he was gone. Though she didn't know exactly what was going on with his illness, David spoke to Nikki every evening for a few months prior to his death. He told her about life. About what to expect. About boys, men, education, religion. He spoke to Nikki about everything that life could throw at her in the future.

Jesse was younger when David was sick, so they couldn't have the same kind of talks that David had with Nikki. Still, David always told Jesse, "You are a tough, smart boy, and you will grow to be a tough, smart man. Be God-fearing, respect women, and protect Mom." Jesse took his advice to heart. You'd think he was Superman the way he tries to protect me. He has a naturally special way of taking care of ladies.

David loved them both so much.

He told me that I'm a tough lady, and I should be proud of myself because I can do things even without him. He wanted me to be strong and continue managing the business and be a good mother and a good citizen in this land of opportunity that he loved.

He'd say, "Life is life. I could be here today and gone tomorrow."

The love of my life lived a full life. He was a happy man. He had everything he always wanted. I'm grateful for what we were able to accomplish together. I know I was only given eighteen years with him, yet we made the best of every single year together.

David believed in God. He always said that we'll meet again in Heaven. And I believe we will.

CHAPTER FOURTEEN

PLANTING SEEDS

THE NORTHERN AND CENTRAL PARTS of Kenya have very different environments. In the north, drought is prevalent, and it's difficult to grow food without a constant water supply. Clean drinking water is even harder to find. In our central part of Kenya, we have trees and the rain forest. We didn't have running water in our homes when I was growing up, but we could regularly find water that could be used for drinking, bathing, washing, etc.

The water supply, in particular, allows the inhabitants of the central part of Kenya to live differently from their countrymen in the north. Growing crops in the north is challenging without water, and finding drinking water requires a nomadic lifestyle. Unfortunately, many people in the north die every year from disease and hunger.

In the area where I grew up, we were able grow food and livestock. The rain forest allowed us to reap abundant harvests to eat or sell. Since we could remain in one place, we built homes and permanent schools, as well as businesses where we could work. These are just a few of the reasons why American missionaries usually help in the northern areas of Kenya instead of where I lived. Many people in my village faced challenges, but they had a better chance of living a stable life because of their farming.

I'm grateful that I've been able to share my blessings with my family and my village in central Kenya. I know that many Kenyan children wish they had what American children have and could do what American children do. But I hope my example shows all Kenyan children that they can and should make use of their blessings to grow spiritually and emotionally. They can empower each other. If they are creative and confident, work hard and have faith in God, they can do just about anything.

When my mom would buy bread, which wasn't often, I would run to our neighbor's house in the morning to share maybe two or three pieces with him and his siblings. Now, the neighbor is a married man with his own kids, and when I visit back home, I buy a few bundles of all-purpose flour to share. We are still friends, and we still share our lives and our treasures with each other, just like my mom taught us to. Mom received and opened her arms to everyone. Her house was always full of people, whether we had something to share or not. That's how I've lived my life too.

My grandmother raised my mom to be a good Christian. Mom will give you anything and everything she owns. She'd say that if she wasn't home and a visitor came, we should offer the visitor whatever we were having. If they didn't want to eat, we should at least give them a glass of water.

When I had money, I'd divide it and send some home. I'd say to my mom, "Give this to my auntie. Give that to the neighbor. Make sure everybody is all set, in terms of basic needs." Basic needs, to me, meant food, a roof on top of them, and medicine. I would tell Mom to divide it up among our friends and family. She did that for me back then, and she still does it now.

I believe that when you do something nice for someone, kindness comes back to you. When I came to America, there was a lady named Carol, who was our neighbor. To tell you the truth, Carol touched me like another angel. My cousin invited me to a wedding, and Carol saw what I was wearing and knew it wouldn't be appropriate. She asked me if I had a dress to wear. I told her no. So she picked me up in her car and took me to a store, where she bought me a long dress, a pair of shoes, and a purse. She was so kind.

I remember how I felt that day, so I have tried to repay her benevolence by helping others. Every once in a while, someone comes to the office and needs help. I offer to take them shopping. We go to the local Walmart store, and I buy them jackets and boots in the wintertime and lighter outfits in the summer. I want to plant a seed. I don't want anything back from them. I don't want them to suffer or get cold or sick. Carol and others assisted me when I came to America, and that's one reason why I keep helping other people who are new to this great country. On a regular basis, I want to pass on the generosity I felt from Carol and others. I plant seeds, and I pray for the seeds to grow.

These days, I employ lots of women as nurses and nurse assistants. My mom taught me how to empower women. She loves to uplift women and so do I. She educates groups at her home about farming. She leads Bible studies and is a peacemaker for her church and village. She even organizes merry-go-round savings groups to show the women what can be done when they work together.

I bet you're wondering what a merry-go-round is! In Kenya women like my mom work but relinquish all of their earnings to their husbands, the heads of the household. The women only receive an allowance for food and basic necessities. They devise ways to save a small portion of each allowance and contribute to a merry-go-round.

Let's say twenty women register for the merry-go-round. Each woman agrees to contribute a specific amount of money every week. For example, they might each present ten dollars to my mom. All the contributions for the week are given to the first woman on the merry-go-round. The woman who receives the lump sum of money uses it to uplift her life. Maybe she'll buy a set of pots she couldn't otherwise afford or clothes for her kids. The next week or month, the money goes to the next woman to uplift her life. That's why it's called a merry-go-round. The pool of money goes from the first woman to the next and to the next, all the way to the last woman in the group.

When my sisters and I were young and it was my mom's turn, she'd sometimes use the money to buy something for our home, like a set of bowls or durable drinking cups or bed sheets, which were all very expensive. Usually, though, she used the money to pay school loans. She would eagerly await that money to pay for something she wouldn't normally have the funds to buy for my sisters and me.

I started a merry-go-round in the Kenyan community when I came to America. It takes a lot of trust, because there are no legal documents to start or run one. Merry-go-rounds are more well known in areas where people, especially women, don't have access to banks or capital. It's kind of like a forced savings account. I don't need to participate anymore, but I know there are some groups that exist today and have helped women buy cars and even put down payments on houses. Merry-go-rounds are very uplifting and do a lot for women in Kenya and in the United States as well.

I learned about generosity from my mom's father too. My grandfather was a good provider, and even though her parents were separated, my mom maintained a positive relationship with her father. He was a chef for the

Norwegian ambassador to Kenya, which was a high-class job that afforded him a very different lifestyle than we lived. He had electricity and lamps (I was amazed by the lampshades) and a beautiful house in the city. I was so excited when my mom visited my grandfather. She'd bring home cupcakes! A cupcake? That was such a treat for us.

My grandfather was also an accomplished businessman who owned a tiny shop after he retired. Whenever I'd get to visit him, he'd send me home with large packages of items—like soap and other necessities—that were destined, originally, for his store's shelves. His grocery gifts were similar to shopping at a big-box membership store in the United States. He was an honest, generous, kind man.

As I've mentioned, my mom invested her money in my education. I was happy, and my sisters were happy for me. I was sad to leave them, and since my mom couldn't pay to educate all of us in a boarding school, I felt like I owed them. I appreciated their sacrifices so much.

I tried to bring back what I learned to teach my sisters and, yes, plant more seeds. For example, the nuns taught me about cleaning, organizing, planning, respect, believing in myself, discipline, resiliency, and much more. They molded me into a tough young woman. Now my sisters tell me they are grateful because I taught them what I learned.

I was living in America when my sisters were in high school. I told my mom that I would send them to any college they wanted to attend. One of the twins went to college for catering and hospitality services. The other twin studied computer skills, and Margaret studied economics. I worked double shifts to pay my bills and to send them each to a four-year college. It wasn't an exceptional amount of money by American college standards, but sending three young women to college felt like a fortune to me.

Josephine is one tough, loving, crazy sister of mine, in a good way. She has the I'm-the-man-of-the-house-but-I'm-a-lady spirit in her. Josephine is particularly protective of Grace, her twin. They don't look alike at all, but my mom used to dress them alike. At least, they were dressed alike until Josephine changed her outfit without my mom knowing. They don't even act the same way, but Josephine can feel when Grace is in pain. She really can feel it. So when we were younger, Margaret and I didn't give Grace a hard time, joke with her too much, or play too hard with her. Josephine would always come in the middle and put us in our place.

Grace never argued. Even up to date, I joke that she was my mom's favorite child, because Mom never disciplined her. Grace usually agreed with everything we said, and if she didn't, she'd have a soft, articulate way of telling us. "You know what? I don't think you should do this. I think you should go this other way."

Since Margaret was the youngest, she basically had no say in anything. She had to agree with Josephine, Grace, and me. Margaret is so successful now. She's raising two kids, drives, has a job, and is well educated. When I go to Kenya, I stay at her house, and she cares for me like a big sister would. When she writes letters thanking me for helping her through college and for my motherly advice, I'm humbled.

I spent a lot of my life away from my sisters. I went to boarding school for primary school, secondary school, and college. I was only home for short vacations between semesters. Then I moved to America. Yet as adult women, we have tight relationships. We talk on a daily or weekly basis. If they want advice, they call me. If I need advice, I call them. Even though we were separated, we experienced a lot as siblings growing up. Mom taught us to always be together, and that's why we are as close as we are even now, thousands of miles apart from each other.

When I wake up in the morning in America, I feel so good. I know that not many people are fortunate to be here, and I feel like I own the world. I'm very, very happy. I'm empowered. I'm brave. I'm resilient. I've overcome a lot. And I want to share everything I've learned and received with everyone I meet.

I'm so grateful for where I live and how God has blessed my life. If I don't share my blessings to help uplift someone else, then I just don't feel right. I'm planting seeds all the time, waiting for a harvest, and counting my own blessings every day. America is beautiful, and freedom is hope. I pray that I'll never take either one for granted and that neither will you.

CHAPTER FIFTEEN

HOPE AND HARD WORK

MOM WOULD GIVE ME A PORTION of land and say, "Shiru, this is your section of the farm. You have to dig all this and make sure we get beans." My sisters would each get their piece of the plot and do the same with a different vegetable. We planted beans, maize, and potatoes, and we even owned a coffee plantation. It was laborious work for kids who weren't yet teenagers, so when we couldn't cover all of it by ourselves, Mom would hire people to help us.

Hard work and hope were staples in my family. My mom always said, "If you work really hard, then you'll be able to reap what you sow. Plant today. Then wait and pray for rain. In a few months, the seed will sprout, and you will harvest." While we waited, Mom taught us to pray and be grateful for the path God created and filled with blessings.

These days, I listen to motivational speakers who have come from nothing to something. They give me the encouragement I need to remember that anything is possible, especially in America. Success almost always requires risk. My mom risked losing time and money when we planted seeds that might not grow, but she always had hope that she'd receive rewards. I have taken so many risks in my life to get where I am today, and I'm grateful that many of those risks bore fruit.

I didn't go for an interview at the Kenyan embassy for my passport and visa. I trusted a woman I barely knew. I gave her my word, and she gave me hers. And somehow, I landed in America with the support of an inspirational group of women.

Even dating David was a risk. I was accustomed to Kenyan men who harassed women and treated women poorly. David wasn't like that, and neither were his friends. I was so blessed to find him and to have him pick me—Walmart ring and all—to spend his life with.

David and I risked everything trying to build a family of our own while he was going through cancer treatments. We were filled with heartbreak when we lost three babies, but we were still hopeful for a healthy family. That hope paid off when our two beautiful miracles were born.

Perhaps the most obvious risk I took was quitting my long-term job at an assisted living facility to go out on my own. Most people in my Kenyan community cautioned me about starting an agency because I wasn't a nurse. They questioned whether I could succeed, but I never did. I was a CNA, and I knew that to be successful I only needed to take care of one person and give that one person the best care possible.

Starting the agency required learning a new set of American procedures, and each step was scary. I didn't (and still don't) want to make a mistake or have someone working for me who makes a mistake that could harm a client or my business' reputation. So I follow up with my employees regularly. I always want to do the right thing in this country.

A new business also required a large down payment for a woman like me at the time. If I failed, I would lose money that I couldn't afford to lose. I refused to fail. I taught myself how to sell my services, so I could pay for the business. I followed the same teachings I learned from my mom. I planted seeds with potential customers and referral partners and hoped I would reap a harvest of clients in the future. Starting a business was risky, and my overwhelming desire to succeed motivated me to take even more risks.

When I began marketing my business, I'd walk into a hospital to give a speech. I'd speak to doctors and lawyers who were educated and intimidating to a woman from Kenya with a partial college education. I was afraid, but I'd go anyway. I'd tell them about the mission that I loved, what I believed in, and that my approach worked. Those talks were hard but necessary to grow my business and build my credibility.

About six months before he passed away, David and I purchased an apartment in the same building we were living in when we got engaged. We rented it out for extra income. Who knew that a girl who grew up in a tiny home with a dirt floor and an outdoor toilet would eventually become a landlord in America? See, there really are no limitations!

We also were interested in purchasing a larger home that was in a better, safer school district. We found a house that we fell in love with, but we halted our plans due to David's illness. While I was in the midst of writing this memoir, I bought the home and moved our family in immediately. Just living this dream that David and I hoped for makes me feel a little closer to him. The apartment and the new house are two of life's little miracles that only occurred because David and I worked hard, hoped, prayed, and never gave up on our dreams. I believed in us. I believed in myself. I believed I could do all I wanted to do.

My belief in myself wasn't negotiable. I not only was on a mission to revolutionize home care, but I also was on a mission to bless my husband. Entrepreneurship is an independent way of providing for your own needs, and I needed to be able to support my family financially so that David could focus on his health. Life can be brutal, and you often have to be braver than you thought possible. When you have an overwhelming reason for doing something you love, you work harder, and you're more committed to succeed. On the day that David resigned from his last job, I knew that I had accomplished my goal.

I want my kids and all the kids in Kenya to know that no human is limited to anything. You can achieve whatever you want if you believe and keep your heart focused on your goal. You should be mindful of what you have and understand that not everyone has the same blessings that you do. Share. Care. Pray. Learn. Be honest. Be authentic. Be positive. Be grateful. Work hard. Plant seeds. Do what you love in life. And believe. You can't go wrong.

Education is the key. My mom chose to educate me, her firstborn. It was a sacrifice, and I appreciate my mom and my sisters so much. Education helped me see what was possible, and it changed my life. I wanted the same opportunities for my sisters, so I chose to educate them with the money that I earned in America. Sure, I could have just sent food and money over to my family and my village, but what will happen when I'm not around anymore? If I send money, my help ends there. If I educate, then the recipients have goodness that lasts in their minds and lives forever.

I think all Kenyan girls should learn how to live independently, and all Kenyan men should learn to respect women. The treatment of women has improved, but there's still more progress to be made. If I had the money, though, I would educate everyone about topics like domestic violence, self-worth, and wealth creation. I'd show them how their lives could be different. My hope is that, by reading my story, people will realize that anything really is possible.

I never knew I would be an American or a landlord or a homeowner or a home care agency owner or a single mother of two amazing children, but I am. And I'm making it work, despite the grief and loss I feel from losing my best friend, my husband. I know I will start my own assisted living or hospice house one day, and my realized vision will be unique and better than any other retirement facility you see today. It will happen with hope and hard work.

Thank God for my husband, David, and the time I had with him. He understood me very well, and he knew I wanted to support my family back in Kenya, as did he. He did his part in paying the bills in America, making sure I was able to support everyone back home. He went above all expectations to make me happy. He loved our children, Nikki and Jesse, more than they will ever realize. And he loved and believed in me more than I was able to repay him. We were a good team, and I'll continue raising our children as honest, God-fearing, grateful American citizens, as I promised him I would.

On Saturday mornings, I treat myself to Dunkin' Donuts hazelnut coffee. I go to the shop, sit, and enjoy my cup. Once, I lived on a coffee plantation but was too poor to have a taste. Now, in America, I have hot coffee every morning, my favorite coffee on Saturdays, and my pick of Kenyan coffee any time I want. For me, coffee is freedom in a cup.

We all get a taste of freedom's little miracles every single day of our lives. I choose to recognize and use my blessings to go beyond all limitations, and I know in my heart that you can too.

We get a taste of
freedom's little
miracles every
single day of our
lives.

CHRONOLOGY

1977 Nancy is born

1987 Nancy's parents separate, and Nancy's mom moves her girls to the farm

1988 Nancy attends St. Theresa's Girls Primary School

1993 Nancy attends Mary Immaculate Girls' Academy

1998 Nancy attends Nyeri Technical College

2001 Nancy's father comes home to the farm

2001 Nancy moves to the United States (August)

2001 Nancy and David go on their first date (Sep 11)

2002 David proposes to Nancy

2002 Nancy receives her CNA certification

2003 Nancy starts working at assisted living facility

2004 David is diagnosed with cancer

2004 Nancy receives Green Card

2006 Nancy goes to Kenya for traditional marriage ceremony and dowry transfer

2009 Nancy becomes a United States citizen

2011 Nancy's father passes away

2011 Nancy resigns from the assisted living facility

2013 David and Nancy marry at Lowell City Hall

2014 Nancy starts Humble Home Care

2019 David passes

2020 Nancy purchases her (and David's) dream home

2020 Nancy publishes her first memoir

GLOSSARY

I love reading because I have the opportunity to build my vocabulary. I like to use my eReader so that I can check the definition of words that are foreign to me. Just in case some of the words I used in this memoir get lost in the translation between English and Swahili, I've included a basic, homemade, glossary of terms.

Ames: See department store.

Big-box store: A store that is set up like a warehouse, and customers purchase a large quantity of the products at a time. Examples: BJs Wholesale Club, Costco, Sam's Club, etc.

Chai (Swahili and English): Tea.

Chemo: See chemotherapy.

Chemo port: A device inserted under the skin (usually the chest) and used to deliver chemotherapy medicines into the patient's bloodstream.

Chemotherapy (also known as chemo): A toxic chemical treatment that selectively destroys deadly cancerous cells but often also destroys healthy cells and causes the patient to experience painful side effects.

Chiggers: Minute parasites about the size of a flea that attach themselves to and feed off a person's skin, causing irritation and discomfort.

Chapati (Swahili): African flatbread.

Clean eating: A dietary practice that advocates for people to eat healthy and whole foods instead of processed, less healthy foods.

Cotton wool: Unprocessed cotton; similar to cotton balls in the United States.

Department store: A large store (in this context, a physical building) in which a wide variety of merchandise is sold.

Disowned: Describes a person who is no longer recognized as having a relationship with the subject. For example, a father disowning his daughter means that the father no longer recognizes a familial relationship with his daughter.

Dress Barn: A women's clothing store.

Florida: A state in the southeast of the United States.

Githeri (Swahili): A cooked mixture of maize and beans.

Green Card: Documentation that confirms a person has permission to reside, permanently, in the United States; also known as a Permanent Resident Card.

Johnny: A lightweight gown that's tied in the back and allows medical professionals to examine patients.

Kayamba (Swahili): A flat instrument like a tray that has seeds inside.

Kenyan shilling: The monetary unit used to pay for goods and services in Kenya. Of course, exchange rates vary over time. I've assumed that one Kenyan shilling (KES) is equivalent to approximately 0.0094 United States dollars (USD) as a consistent standard for this book.

Kitenge (Swahili): A fancy dress that wraps around your body like a sarong.

Maize (Swahili): Corn.

Massachusetts: A state in the northeast of the United States.

Matutu (Swahili): A taxi cab or van.

McDonald's: An American fast food restaurant that sells inexpensive burgers, french fries, and chicken nuggets.

Misogynistic: A type of behavior or attitude that supports the hatred, mistreatment, and/or abuse of women.

Mtungi (Swahili): A container, jar, or pitcher for carrying liquids. Kenyan women tied mtungis filled with water on their backs to carry water from the source to their homes.

Muzungu (Swahili): Name for a Caucasian person.

Nairobi: The capital city of Kenya.

Per diem: Paying by the day. If you are paid per diem, you are paid for each day that you work; you are not paid a lump sum of money for the whole month.

Pilau (Swahili): A rice and spices dish.

Port: See chemo port.

Radiation (also known as radiation therapy): A process by which concentrated energy particles are beamed into a patient's body in an effort to destroy deadly cancer cells. This process often causes painful side effects.

Remission: A temporary or permanent period during which a patient's cancer is dormant or lessened.

Swahili: Kenya's predominant language.

Texas: A state in the south-central area of the United States near the Mexican border.

Walmart: See department store.

Made in the USA
Columbia, SC
15 September 2020